"Ebony has done a remarkable job in both research and insight into the rising influence of Eastern Mysticism, introduced through Yoga, into Western culture, and more specifically, the Western church.

The book of Isaiah 2:6 prophesied concerning Israel that, as a nation, God was lifting his hedge of protection over them because they had become polluted with influences from the east.

The Church at Corinth was well known for, and marked by, the depth of their encounter with the power of the Holy Spirit, and the grace gifting that subsequently accompanied their experience. Yet, the Apostle Paul wrote to them of his concern in 2 Corinthians 11:4 that they were in danger of receiving another spirit that would pull them away from their pure devotion to Christ.

I would encourage anyone who needs an excellent resource for insight into this growing, influential movement to read about Ebony's experience and the inherent danger of following the path of Yoga."

Tim and Cindy McGill

Ministry leaders, teachers, and speakers; Cindy is also an author and the founder of Freedom Lounge.

"Ebony is a God breathed wonder! The words she has written stem from her deep love and reverence for God. This book is a direct reflection of every precious promise from the Bible she has tucked away in her heart. Whether it is people, places, or things, Ebony has used each life experience, including her quest for true peace, serenity, and contentment, to further deepen her intimacy with God. Her relationship with God is the foundation of everything her Heavenly Father has called her to be. I am so very proud of her."

Leah Conedy

First Lady, teacher, speaker

MIND BODY SPIRIT

God's Way

THE UNRAVELING THAT REVEALED
I WASN'T A YOGI AFTER ALL

EBONY CLAYTON

FIRST EDITION

To my God, my Lord and Savior, my Teacher and my Comforter: Thank you for encouraging me to share my testimony. For every heart that is turned, You get all the glory, honor, and praise.

To my Husband: Thank you for your encouragement, your support, your prayers, your feedback, and your love.

To my baby girl, my biggest cheerleader: Thank you for hyping me up and praying for mommy. I love you.

To every woman I once encouraged to embrace yoga. To those who followed my lead, found inspiration in my words, my posts, or my presence, this book is for you: I write with a repentant heart, acknowledging that, in my ignorance, I promoted a path that does not honor God. Let my testimony be a correction and a call back to the narrow way.

TABLE OF CONTENTS

INTRODUCTION

Hi, hello, and welcome. My name is Ebony, and I'm a recovering yogi.

I chuckled as I wrote that because this sentence, although genuinely sincere, is also highly misleading at the same time. It sounds like I've just returned from some intense detox program, doesn't it? I guess in some ways, it was a detox, which in turn makes me feel like I may have been addicted. Maybe I was. I eventually reached the point where I attended yoga class daily, sometimes twice a day, but there was no 12-step program to help me wean myself off sun salutations and warrior stances. In reality, it was much more nuanced than that. The "addiction" wasn't necessarily harmful; it was a passion. I love to exercise, but I'm not really a "go to the gym and lift weights" kind of girl. I prefer a class setting that promotes movement, such as dance, stretching, or similar group fitness class, so I thought I had found my thing in yoga. I was in the best shape of my life, and it felt amazing! I loved the calmness it brought into my life during a traumatic time, the flexibility I felt in my body, the sense of community it provided, and the constant push I felt to be better than I was the day before. I guess it was, in fact, addictive.

That was the ignorant side of my relationship with yoga. Over time, I learned I wasn't really into "yoga." And I don't mean that in the way gym goers say, "I hate the gym but love the results." I mean, I was not a yogi by any means, despite what my social media posts might suggest. I wasn't into yoga, at least not in the way I thought I was, and that's because at the time, I didn't really know what yoga was.

I can practically hear the questions forming in your mind: "Wait! How can you attend classes daily and rave about the results yet simultaneously not be into it? And moreover, how could you not know what you were into?"

I know that sounds counterintuitive, but it's the facts, and I will explain more as I attempt to share my journey with you. The term "recovering yogi" might sound a bit dramatic, but it perfectly captures my process of stepping away. It explains how allowing God to speak into every area of my life eradicated compromise, which in turn kept my relationship with God at the forefront.

A little more about me will help set the stage. I'm a wife to my love and an adoptive mommy to the sweetest, most determined little girl; I'm a survivor of trauma; I'm a clinician, mindset coach, and group fitness instructor; I'm a plant mom and an adventurer that loves to travel, bike, hike, explore, and my new pastime: hammocking; I'm a wannabe singer (off-key but on-point), a multi-passionate creative, and a minimalist except for my closet; I'm what one would consider counter-cultural; I'm a little old school, a little new school, and a little free spirit; basically, if I could sum all of this up in one sentence, it would be, I wasn't created to be put in a box. There have been times in my life when I fought against this reality, but once I realized God made me this way, I accepted myself for who I am. Once I realized I'm multifaceted, like a diamond, it was easier to accept. I'm sparkly and extra. It's my personality. The essential part is that all my facets are submitted to the will of God and open to His rebuke. God is the most important part of my life, and let me get specific here because so many people use "God" to describe the object of their affections or the thing that's bigger than them, but I am a child of who I believe to be the one and only God, a follower of Jesus, and a lover of His Holy Spirit.

Why do I share all this? Well, first, I want to give you a glimpse into my reality, because all these things don't usually go together. I'm kind of used to being an outlier, different, and the weird one in my circle. So, going against the grain is not outside of the norm for me. And second, I share this to set the stage for this book. I've never really fit into a mold, so when I received a little pushback after deciding to start taking yoga classes with my friend a little over fifteen years ago, I wasn't automatically persuaded to stop doing yoga. If you're asking, "Pushback from whom?", it was from fellow believers in Christ! And as a believer myself, I share that with no ill intent (I'm writing a book about them being right), but at the time, it felt like judgmentalism. I brushed it off because we all know people are people, Christian or otherwise, and that sometimes means dealing with things like judgmentalism, racism, ageism, classism, sexism, and many other " isms." At the time, I felt these were the people who had the biggest opinions yet couldn't back them up. I was hit with the "You shouldn't practice yoga," yet no one could give me an answer that felt worthy of stopping, so I continued because to me, it was "only exercise."

I also received pushback regarding yoga just because it was different and outside of the norm for people in my community. Still, I felt like I had always received pushback from others, so it wasn't uncommon for me. Occasionally, I would hear, "Yoga isn't Christian," but I knew that God knew my heart, and I wasn't there for the "spiritual" side of yoga anyway; therefore, I thought that didn't apply to me. Again, I was only there for the exercise. And could that be wrong, especially when the results were so right?

In 1 Corinthians 10, Paul uses the story of the Israelites wandering through the wilderness as a bright, flashing warning sign—**DANGER!** He didn't share this just for the sake of history, but He was urging us to pay attention to their story so we don't repeat their mistakes. Their journey is written down for us, like road signs guiding us away from the pitfalls that caused them to stumble. It's the love of God that gives us these warnings, and it's not to scare us, but to keep us safe. God is showing us that we don't have to touch the fire to know it's hot. The message is clear: *Don't get burned.* Learn from their mistakes. It's as if God is holding up a bright neon sign that says, "Fire burns!" He's lovingly reminding us that the consequences of wandering off the path that leads to Him are just as painful as getting burned. I've learned in this life that you don't need to feel the heat to believe the fire is real. Heed the warnings, and you can avoid the blisters and scars that come from playing too close to the flames.

But let's be real for a second. You "could" ignore the signs. You "could" try to experience everything on your own. But doesn't that sound like the hard way? We don't need to walk down every dead-end path or suffer every painful consequence to learn valuable lessons. God, in His wisdom and kindness, has given us the experiences and stories of those who have gone before us. My experience at my yoga teacher training is a giant red flag signaling, "Stop! Don't go this way!" Use my experience as a warning to protect yourself.

The truth is, it's easy to get caught up in things that feel good in the moment. We live in a world that encourages us to chase after self-fulfillment, to pursue things on our own terms, and to seek out new experiences that promise peace or power, but let me remind you that not every road leads to God. The Bible warns us repeatedly to be cautious. There are ways of thinking and living that can seem appealing and harmless at first, but will ultimately lead us straight into deception. And that deception has one goal: to pull us away from the God who loves us and knows what is best for us.

In this book, I hope to share my story and my heart. I want my sisters in Christ to be aware of the subtle ways that culture and "spirituality" can infiltrate their faith. My goal is to encourage Christian women in the mind-body-spiritual health space to think critically when making wellness choices, as this space has become increasingly influenced by New Age perspectives. It is possible to pursue health in body, mind, and spirit without compromising your faith. Deception is real, and the enemy will use any means at his disposal. It's not just about yoga. It's about spiritual discernment, obedience, and letting God draw the line.

We must remain vigilant. We must be on guard against anything that prioritizes self over God or promises enlightenment apart from Him. These things will not be overtly displayed on banners, they are more subtle and unveil themselves over time. It's so easy to be led astray when we let our guard down. Scripture is the compass that points us toward God, and away from paths that lead into the traps of the enemy. If we keep our eyes on Jesus, we can navigate this world without falling into the traps that have ensnared so many. God's warnings are not meant to restrict us but to protect us. Just as a loving parent warns their child not to touch a hot stove, God's Word is full of loving reminders to steer clear of danger. Heed God's wisdom. Don't test the fire for yourself. Stay close to Him, follow the signs He's placed before you (even if that's someone else's experience), and trust that His way is the best way, the safest way, and most importantly, the ONLY way if you desire life and godliness.

Now, come along with me as we learn what it really means to be a "Yogi."

PART ONE:

My Yoga Journey

YOGA TEACHER TRAINING THROUGH A BIBLICAL WORLDVIEW

The beginning of my story started when I learned that religion and relationship were two very different things and that being connected to God started with me saying yes to Jesus. But the beginning of this particular part of my story began when I really started to immerse myself in yoga classes as a coping mechanism. It then progressed into me pursuing a desire to combine my love for yoga with my mental health practice, so I decided to pursue a yoga teacher certification. I really felt like I was on to something. I wanted to create a space where I wasn't just referring people to take classes, but providing a space where they could take them. Yoga is a common recommendation of many different types of practitioners as an intervention to work alongside their treatment. Counselors recommend yoga as an additional tool for the treatment of anxiety, depression, trauma, and stress-related disorders. Physicians recommend it as a holistic approach to health and wellness. Physical therapists either recommend or incorporate yoga into their regimen to help patients recovering from injuries. Personal trainers might recommend yoga to increase flexibility. Nutritionists, dieticians, massage therapists, life coaches, and wellness advocates may talk to their clients about the benefits of yoga. That's a lot of people pushing yoga. Some of them probably have a complete understanding of what yoga is and what it is not, but I would venture to say that most recommend yoga without a full picture of what it really is. I'm here to share with you what yoga actually is and hopefully open your eyes to what's going on underneath all the "stretching."

I'm here to share with you what yoga actually is and hopefully open your eyes to what's going on underneath all the "stretching."

I remember the first day of yoga teacher training as if it were yesterday. I was so excited to take my practice to the next level. With my textbooks in hand and a fresh notebook covered in mandalas (which I later learned is a geometric figure in Hinduism that represents the universe), I was ready to go. The excitement was embedded in naivety, but that's the best kind, isn't it?

Our first assignment was to write about what we hoped to gain from the experience. What was our goal? Here's what I wrote on the first page of my notebook on my first day of class:

"Here I am at yoga teacher training. My first day! Wow. Thank you, God, for this opportunity. Yoga, I believe, will bring patience, alignment, flexibility, and stillness not only in my body but in my day-to-day life and in my walk with You. I wanted to do this for my physical health, but I believe You will use this to teach me so much more. This year has been about the alignment of my mind, body, and spirit. This is just one more step in that direction. My goals for this training are:

More stillness in my practice and my poses.

Learning about my body by being safe, learning proper alignment, when to push, and when to be still.

Increased flexibility and, most of all, having patience with myself.

Yoga is not about perfection. It's about perseverance. If I fall out of something, I'll get back in. If my body doesn't allow me to do something today, maybe it will tomorrow. It's about keeping the faith, continuing to try, never giving up, accepting the now, and being in the moment."

So, here I am about to state the obvious. I hope you noticed my response to our very first assignment in my yoga teacher training was a prayer. I never imagined the fourth sentence would hold such a prophetic undertone: "I believe You will use this to teach me so much more." That was 100% true! I hope you also noticed that I had my own definition of yoga. I tried to dictate what yoga was, but I was about to discover its true definition.

I entered this endeavor with God at the forefront, as I try to do with everything in my life. Sitting in a yoga class and praying was not uncommon for me, as my entire practice was built around making God my spiritual connection during yoga. Yet there was always this underlying discomfort during certain classes that I would dismiss by focusing on God. That's what I want to talk about. I want to share how a Holy Spirit-filled, Christ-centered, Jesus-loving woman of God found herself opening doors to the New Age belief system by "just exercising."

Picture this: It's now my second day of yoga teacher training. I'm sitting in class, excited to learn, eager to grow, ready to get in better shape than before. I'm coming off the high of day one, and the excitement is still fresh. This is our first real lesson. The instructor is scheduled to start with the *Yoga Sutras.* My face is beaming. Let's do this! I'm about to be a certified yoga instructor, yay! She begins to share that the *Yoga Sutras,* or yogic scriptures, as they are called, are a collection of ancient Hindu texts that serve as the foundational philosophy of classical yoga. Wait! Hindu texts? I said to myself, *I thought yoga wasn't a religion.* Then, the Holy Spirit chimed in and reminded me that I bought most of my required books for class from the bookstore's religion section. Here is where I first started to feel a little uncomfortable. Not enough to say anything or leave, but just enough to become a little more aware of what was being taught. I continued to listen. The instructor went on to discuss the belief that the Sutras were written by the sage Patanjali, who, based on her explanation, may or may not have existed. Okay, let's pause for a second. I literally looked around the class at this point to see if anyone else heard that. No one else batted an eye. No one responded. Everyone just kept listening, as if she hadn't said what she just said.

The instruction continued, so I continued listening, but my ears were definitely open. The instructor then opened her mouth and nonchalantly uttered her next sentence, almost highlighting it as an interesting tidbit of information. She shared, "Patanjali is translated as 'fallen angel.'" Um, what? Again, my eyes scanned the room, but more vigorously this time than the last. I looked to the left and right, my mind racing with the thought, *Is anyone else actually listening to what's being said?* I felt like the only person in the room with eyes and ears wide open. I remember my brain going into overdrive and doing a little translation of its own: "Fallen angel? That – is – a – demon! What is going on here? Is anyone else picking up what she's putting down?"

The Fall of Lucifer
Isaiah 14:12-15 (NKJV)

"How you are fallen from heaven, O Lucifer, son of the morning! How you are cut down to the ground, you who weakened the nations! For you have said in your heart: 'I will ascend into heaven, I will exalt my throne above the stars of God; I will also sit on the mount of the congregation On the farthest sides of the north; I will ascend above the heights of the clouds, I will be like the Most High.' Yet you shall be brought down to Sheol, to the lowest depths of the Pit."

Satan Thrown Out of Heaven
Revelation 12:7-12 (NKJV)

"And war broke out in heaven: Michael and his angels fought with the dragon; and the dragon and his angels fought, but they did not prevail, nor was a place found for them in heaven any longer. So the great dragon was cast out, that serpent of old, called the Devil and Satan, who deceives the whole world; he was cast to the earth, and his angels were cast out with him.

Then I heard a loud voice saying in heaven, 'Now salvation, and strength, and the kingdom of our God, and the power of His Christ have come, for the accuser of our brethren, who accused them before our God day and night, has been cast down. And they overcame him by the blood of the Lamb and by the word of their testimony, and they did not love their lives to the death. Therefore rejoice, O heavens, and you who dwell in them! Woe to the inhabitants of the earth and the sea! For the devil has come down to you, having great wrath, because he knows that he has a short time.'"

Patanjali is often portrayed as half human and half serpent, and during additional research I later discovered that there is an invocation used to summon this spirit.[1] I was already on high alert before learning that information. *How is this exercise?* This question kept ringing in my head.

That marked a turnaround moment, or at least the beginning of a turnaround for me. The excitement I felt on that first day and the start of the second was almost gone. The red flags were waving. I remember this day, and as I reflect, I realize how strongly the Holy Spirit was convicting my spirit. My spidey senses were on overdrive, yet I continued to acknowledge and dismiss, acknowledge and dismiss. I acknowledged the discomfort and was aware of it, but I continued to dismiss it and tried to make myself comfortable in my conviction, ignoring my discernment. All of this is hindsight 20/20 because these weren't my thoughts at the moment, and that's not how conviction is supposed to work, right? We're supposed to turn away from the thing God is convicting us of, not soothe ourselves out of the conviction so we can continue on with our regularly scheduled programming. I am so thankful God is always with us and will never leave us or forsake us (Deuteronomy 31:8); even in our ignorance and stupidity, God causes everything to work together for the good of those who love Him and are called according to His purpose (Romans 8:28). He just kept on speaking to me each day, as you will soon see.

The *Yoga Sutras* lessons continued. The instructor shared that the *Sutras* consist of 196 aphorisms that teach the principles and practices of yoga. They provide a philosophical framework and practical guidance for understanding the nature of the mind, the practice of yoga, and the path toward spiritual awakening.

Here, I'd like to share more about the yogic scriptures so that you can have an understanding of their role. The Sutras make up the whole ideology of yoga – they are what most yoga teachers draw from when teaching their classes at your local gym or private studio. The little phrases, the encouraging parables, the inspiring lessons, the intentions they encourage you to set – the Sutras are the basis. Even if teachers say they don't use the *Yoga Sutras,* they must learn about them in order to receive a certification to teach. So each yoga teacher is fully aware of these yogic scriptures.

The *Yoga Sutras* are comprised of four chapters that cover different aspects of yoga. I'm going to lay out a brief summary of each in the Appendix if you're interested in seeing what each person who goes through yoga teacher training must learn and understand about the practice before they are certified.

I won't go through all of them, but I want to shine a spotlight on the first two:

- The first sutra is Samadhi Pada. It teaches that the ultimate goal of yoga, meaning "to yoke" or "union", is to reach a state of deep meditation where a person feels completely one with the divine, and the physical postures (asanas) are designed to prepare them for this union.[2]

- The second sutra is Sadhana Pada. It lays out the eight limbs of Yoga. It's the guide for spiritual growth, from ethical living and physical postures (asanas) to meditation and ultimately, unity with the universe. Each limb marks a step toward self-realization.[2]

In the first two sutras, you learn that there's no such thing as isolating exercise from the whole of yoga – but if you aren't convinced yet, that's okay. I didn't see it at first either, and it didn't click for me until much later.

Okay, so let's back up and focus on how I responded to hearing all this in class. Learning more about the Sutras and who Patanjali really was began to bother me. I mean, this was yoga history–the foundation of what it means to practice yoga–and more importantly, this was only day two. What was I getting myself into?

If you're reading this and have completed yoga teacher training, how did you reconcile this in your spirit during the training? I was a little shocked when we got to this point. I remember my eyes widening more and more in disbelief and my heart racing as I took notes. I wanted to ensure that I was capturing all this information, as I subconsciously knew it would be applied in more ways than just for the sake of my certification. However, I wasn't sure in what ways. I remember calling my friend after each class and saying, "Girl, guess what I learned today?!"

Speaking of friends, there was one girl in my class I connected with. We were sitting near each other, she seemed friendly, and she was the only other person of color in the class; we seemed to naturally connect. I later found out that she was a professing "Christian" as well, so we buddied up and became each other's encouragement and eventual friends. During a break, I leaned over and asked her what she thought about what we were learning. Truth be told, I was fishing. I really wanted to know if she felt as uncomfortable as I did. This is where I felt led to open up about my concerns. I shared what we had just learned that stuck out to me. Her response was confirming and somewhat eased my mind. She said, "I'm just here to get my certificate, and that's it!" *Okay*, I thought, *I can get behind that*. It was exactly how I felt. I wasn't there for all the extra stuff. I just wanted my certificate so I could teach the way I wanted to teach. I had no plans on bringing all the stuff they were teaching into my practice.

Side note: Isn't it funny how we try to find people to agree with what we feel is right rather than just leaning into which way the Holy Spirit is directing us to go? Just me? Okay. Let me continue.

We then began to discuss how, once we received our certification, we would make our yoga practice our own. She shared her vision for her yoga practice, and I shared mine. I was re-energized and ready to take on the rest of the class.

On day three, we briefly discussed chakras, energy centers believed to exist within people, as found in the teachings of Hinduism, Buddhism, and the New Age movement. Chakras are, of course, not taught in Christianity, making this yet another moment in class that had me rolling my eyes.

The days went on, and I kept my focus. I knew this was all outside of my deeply held Christian beliefs, but I was determined to stay the course and power through to get my certificate and make my yoga practice Christian, with the intent of teaching my Christian version of yoga to other believers.

As time went on, we continued to go over more principles and beliefs, the Sutras, and so on. Don't get me wrong, it wasn't all blatantly anti-Christian or demonic in nature, some of the philosophies and beliefs aligned with my own. Yoga and Biblical beliefs share some similarities, including self-reflection, introspection, personal growth, morality, treating others with kindness and respect, charitable acts, spiritual connectedness, and seeking wisdom. It was during this time that God began to speak to me about deception and how it really works. He showed me that there is always truth in deception. There has to be. No one is going to connect with a complete, total, and obvious lie; there has to be something you agree with that draws you in, and that's where the enemy has an open door. We'll talk about deception in more depth later on.

If you're wondering if we did anything other than talk about the belief system of yoga, we did. Among all the religious teachings, we were taking yoga classes, which didn't contain any of the material we were learning. They were normal yoga classes, which included: asanas–the exercises of yoga, and an occasional 'namaste' –a traditional greeting, and 'intention setting,'. What happens in each class, however, really depends on the teacher. In addition, we were also learning how to teach yoga.

Many parts of the overall training were uncomfortable at times, but the feeling of discomfort was not constant. We had to learn the sequencing of the asanas, which is why I was really there. These are the movements or exercises, it's what people usually picture when they think of yoga. The asanas are essential, but they're only a small part of the bigger picture. Remember, according to the *Yoga Sutras*, asanas are only intended to prepare the body and mind for the higher stages of meditation and spiritual growth.[2] I'll take this opportunity to also remind you who wrote the *Yoga Sutras* (or the yogic scriptures), Patanjali (whose name, don't forget, translates to "fallen angel"). That still blows my mind!

Think about it like this. Yoga is kind of like training for a long-distance run. Stretching is important, but the goal isn't just to master the perfect stretch. The goal is to build endurance and strength for the long race ahead. The asanas act in the same way. They are just preparation. They are a warm-up for the more advanced stages of yoga. The deeper aspects of yoga focus on mastering the mind, controlling your breath, withdrawing from distractions, and eventually, achieving a union with the divine; at least, that's what the original texts say. The watered-down, Western version of yoga teaches that it's just exercise, but what's often glossed over is that it's a spiritual practice, and with that, spiritual danger creeps in.

Patanjali's teachings advocate for a type of enlightenment that seeks union with the universe or the original energy, rather than with the God of the Bible. So while someone might be drawn to yoga for the physical benefits, it's crucial to be aware of the spiritual path the practice leads toward, according to its ancient roots. It's not just stretching; it's preparing your body and mind for something more, something that will ultimately lead you away from God's truth.

There are eight limbs in yoga, found in book 2 of the *Yoga Sutras*, and the asanas (exercises) are number three. I won't bore you with a detailed description of each limb of yoga because I have something much more surprising to reveal, but here's the list for reference:[2]

1. Yama (ethical principles)

2. Niyama (self-discipline and observances)

3. Asana (physical postures, the "exercises")

4. Pranayama (breath control, breathwork)

5. Pratyahara (withdrawal of the senses)

6. Dharana (concentration)

7. Dhyana (meditation)

8. Samadhi (state of oneness, no separation between self and the universe)

Now, let's go back to the lecture portion of class. I'm not sure what day this was, but we're definitely getting closer to me questioning if I should continue obtaining my certification. At this point, I was still taking as many notes as possible, knowing I'd be sharing this information with others. We were all sitting in a circle, notebooks out, handouts within reach, as the instructor was in the midst of the lesson. That day's topic was the *moola bandha*. I don't remember exactly, but knowing me, I probably rolled my eyes, again, thinking, *Great! The moola bandha! What's this going to be about?* I was not expecting what came next.

As the instructor went on, I listened intently. I learned that the moola bandha is a yogic technique that involves engaging and activating the "root lock" or "moola bandha" in the body. It's part of the practice of Kundalini yoga. This is where I was taken aback. The instructor, in her true fashion, without blinking an eye, said Kundalini is all about breathwork, with the idea being to awaken dormant spiritual energy known as Kundalini. I know my facial expressions were saying all that needed to be said; I'm not sure if she saw me or not.

The instructor went on to "educate" us by sharing that, according to yogic philosophy, there is a dormant serpent energy that is coiled at the base of the spine, and it's through the breathwork of Kundalini that serpent energy is released into the body. It was at this point that my arm shot up like an elementary schooler who was excited to have the right answer. I said in my most declarative tone, "I don't have any serpent energy at the base of my spine." Her response was unremarkable, but I didn't need a response. I only needed to break the zombie-like devotion that was in the room. Everyone was okay with what was being said. My statement was more of an announcement. I was internally thinking, *Oh no, no, no, NO. There is no serpent energy here. The only "energy" in me is the power of the Holy Spirit.* I looked around the room, feeling like there was a veil over the minds of everyone listening. It seemed like they were blind to every word. No one questioned anything; they just accepted it as their spiritual truth. Christian or not, I thought it weird to just believe someone who tells you that you have the energy of a serpent bound up inside you, waiting to be released.

Now, you may wonder if this was the final straw that led to me walking away. Unfortunately, no. You see, Kundalini is just a type of yoga, and even though I had such a strong response, my thought process at the time went a little like this: *There are many different types of yoga, so I'll just steer clear of Kundalini. Boom! Problem fixed; crisis averted. No Kundalini yoga for me, so I'm in the clear.*

Thinking back to that time, there were many things I allowed myself to be "okay with" in order to receive my certification and "make yoga my own." Hindsight is always 20/20, and looking back, I can see the compromises. At the moment, I felt I was protecting my spirit, but I now know I was justifying. I was putting up with a lot in order to reach the point where I could be certified and do yoga my way, as if there were a "my way." I still hadn't fully grasped what yoga really was; that came afterwards, while researching, but all the while, God was preparing me for the realization that I would not be continuing the journey as I thought I would.

YOGA IS NOT STRETCHING

*"Yoga is not about touching your toes; it is what
you learn on the way down." – Jigar Gor*

This widely used quote in the world of yoga emphasizes that
the true value of yoga does not lie in the poses themselves,
but in the personal growth that unfolds during your practice.
Well, for me, I learned quite a bit.

A little over halfway through the class, we had a guest speaker
scheduled for a philosophy workshop. The guest speaker was a
seasoned yogi and instructor who specialized in yoga philosophy
with an emphasis on pranayama (breathwork) and meditation.
It was during his workshop that I felt a palpable shift in the
atmosphere.

I remember that day vividly – it was the last Sunday in October. This was the day that would become the ultimate turning point. This was the moment that illuminated everything I had been learning up until that point in time. This was the day that everything clicked into place, and it all made sense. Journey with me.

We started the day talking about the different schools of yoga regarding the paths to achieve soul union. Even writing "soul union" makes me think, *really, Ebony?* Using words like "soul union" wasn't enough? I do think about how much I downplayed things. It grieves my spirit. I think about when Paul says, "A little leaven works through the whole batch of dough" in Galatians 5:9 (BSB). A little bit of leaven, a slight leaning into error, affected me as a whole. I found myself accepting ideas, language, and actions that now sound crazy to me. I thank God that my ear was attuned to His voice and in the midst of my confusion, He was right by my side, because He never leaves or forsakes us (Deuteronomy 31:6, ESV, paraphrased). And, "All of us like sheep have gone astray, we have turned, each one, to his own way; but the Lord has caused the wickedness of us all [our sin, our injustice, our wrongdoing] to fall on Him [instead of us]" (Isaiah 53:6 AMP). May I forever be in awe of the love of the gospel. I digress.

Back to the different schools of yoga. Mentioning the different schools of yoga is important to know here in the West because we treat yoga like a gym membership. There are many kinds of yoga practices incorporated into a class, depending on the instructor's school of thought, personal practice, teaching style, and the studio's overall viewpoint. All of yoga is a spiritual practice, but I've provided a list in the Appendix of different types of yoga and their meanings. If you've taken any kind of yoga class, you've sat under the spirit of Hinduism.

I know I already spoke of Kundalini yoga, but I want to highlight it here once again because this was the one our guest instructor spent extra time cautioning us on. I wrote his words down in my journal verbatim. Take a look:

"If you would like to reference number three, it highlights that the fire/serpent energy can be dangerous."

> *If you've taken any kind of yoga class, you've sat under the spirit of Hinduism.*

Number three was Kundalini, and it was described to us in this way: the fire or serpent energy that lies dormant, coiled at the base of your spine, waiting to be awakened. This energy, once released into your body through breathwork, is said to grant the yogi extraordinary powers, including but not limited to psychic abilities, astral travel, and other supernatural gifts. But in the midst of the description outlined on the worksheet, we were cautioned to "be careful." And, this "caution" was from a seasoned yogi who has devoted their life to the practice of yoga. Why attach a caution sign to something you believe is good for you? This wasn't a "it's good for you in moderation" caution like with dark chocolate. It was more of a be careful because this could get dangerous caution.

He then began to share accounts of individuals who, upon awakening this "energy," began to lose their grip on reality and started "going crazy," "hearing voices," and experiencing other supernatural phenomena. I remember feeling so uncomfortable. This was not what I signed up for. This wasn't just about stretching or meditation anymore. Does this sound like "just exercise" to you? It didn't to me. It was a disturbing atmosphere, at least for me, but I'm sure there were people who felt right at home. To me, it felt more like the final straw. I remember thinking, it doesn't matter that I don't plan on engaging in Kundalini or any Kundalini practices. The Holy Spirit had been sending blaring warning bells over the past several weeks, and finally, I reached the point where the ringing in my mind was solidified, and the time to take action was now.

There I was in class, rethinking it all. Questioning myself. Wondering why I didn't dig deeper sooner. Realizing there was no making yoga my own or saying "God knows my heart" in order to excuse my behavior. I realized that I couldn't keep reciting, what I now call my "justifying Bible verse", from 1 John, "Greater is He who is in me than He who is in the world," just to ease my mind and allow me to sit in a class that felt off from the beginning (1 John 4:4 NKJV, paraphrased). I was coming to grips with the fact that me using the phrase, "I'm not here for the spiritual side of yoga; I'm just here for the exercise," was a poor explanation to convince myself that it was okay, and using the phrase, "When I get certified, I can make it Christian" was a terrible defense. It was all just crazy talk.

Now, I didn't jump up, make a scene, grab my things, and run out. Maybe I should have, but I just sat there, thinking, *This is crazy! How did I end up in this environment learning about New Age practices, and not just for myself, but with the goal being to teach others and encourage them in this? I never thought I'd be in this space!*

Okay, back to class. It continued on, despite my deep introspection, mulling over all my regrets, and trying to figure out how I arrived sitting on the floor, criss-cross applesauce, in a room full of the spirit of the Antichrist. That might seem like an exaggerated statement, but the spirit of the Antichrist is operating in anyone or in any place where Christ is opposed or denied, and that's where I was sitting. Right smack dab in the middle of it, and not as a light in a dark place.

I was pulled out of my thoughts by one of my cohorts when he blurted out a question that caused the guest speaker to respond in an annoyed and somewhat condescending way. Looking back, I wonder if my cohort was also questioning their journey. I'll never know, but the guest speaker definitely made it known that it was a strange question at that point in the class. Either way, I'm so glad he asked because I got to witness the response he was given firsthand.

I was done at this point anyway, but when I heard what the instructor said, I was really done. My fellow cohort asked what I'm sure many Christians, myself included, ask themselves, "Is it possible for someone to practice yoga just for the asanas?" The guest speaker answered him swiftly and abruptly in a tone that seemed aggressive and militant. He barked back, "If you don't realize by this point that there is no separation of the asanas from the rest of yoga, you are in the wrong place." It was most definitely a mic drop moment. It was the final nail, the last straw, whatever idiom you choose that signifies THE END.

Speaking of the end, let's jump headfirst into the deep end. It took me a little more than half of a 10-week program to get it. I cringe inside saying that, but God used that time to educate me so I can educate you. Here we go. I walked away from yoga teacher training realizing that: **Yoga is not JUST stretching.**

Even though I felt like I had wasted weeks of my time, a lot of my money, and a form of movement that felt good to my body and that I thoroughly enjoyed, I found myself grateful for this workshop. It provided clarity amid uncertainty.

Suddenly, everything I learned took on a different weight. This class was not just about improving my personal practice, the benefits of exercise or flexibility, finding inner peace, or learning to teach others to do the same. What I was being taught was not something that aligned with my faith or Biblical principles, and God's Holy Spirit made that very evident. My goal to get others to practice yoga turned into a goal to share all the reasons why my sisters in Christ shouldn't, because yoga is not just stretching.

Before discussing what yoga is in the next chapter, I want to share a direct quote from The *Yoga Sutras* of Patanjali taken from the first paragraph of the introduction.

"When the word Yoga is mentioned, most people immediately think of some physical practices for stretching and stress reduction. This is one aspect of the Yogic science, but actually only a very small part and relatively recent in development.[2]"

What most people call yoga is just the tip of the iceberg. I didn't create this message; rather, I am shedding light on aspects that are not openly discussed during an hour-long yoga class. Unless you seek out this information yourself, it can easily remain hidden in the shadows.

SO WHAT IS YOGA THEN?

Yoga is a belief system. It's a philosophy. It's a way of being. It's a lifestyle. I would say it's a faith system, not a formal religion, but definitely a spiritual practice that one has to put their faith in. **Yoga is NOT exercise**. Yoga is a spiritual practice with a physical component, not the other way around. I'll say it another way: yoga is not physical exercise with a spiritual component you get to opt out of; the exercise part of yoga, the asanas, are just one small subsection.

Remember the definition of the word "yoga." It means to unite or join, and it's derived from the Sanskrit word "yuj," which means "to yoke.[1]" To yoke? I don't know how you just reacted, but the first time I heard that in class, my initial thought was, *Yoke to what? What exactly are we yoking to?* I'm sure the expression on my face was like, Huh?, like you're about to ask a question but are too stunned to form words. It's that frozen-in-confusion look that says, *Wait... run that by me again?*

The practice of yoga originated in India and has deep connections to Hinduism, as well as influences from Buddhism and Jainism. If you study enough about yoga, you'll realize that it has been culturally appropriated to sell classes and merchandise to suburban Americans.

I remember watching a cooking show on Netflix quite a few years after my yoga teacher training experience, and it really solidified what the Lord showed me in that class. The show was about a chef that would go and visit restaurants around the world with the goal of highlighting cultural influences. This particular episode took place in India, and he featured a famous Indian actress as a guest who had much to say about the practice of yoga in America. She expressed her concern about the commercialization of yoga, it not being respected for the spiritual practice it is, and voiced her desire for people to do their homework and truly study the Indian culture.[2]

Yoga teacher training teaches that the practices, postures, and techniques of yoga are designed to promote a physical, mental, and spiritual connection by yoking with the atman (individual soul) and the Brahman (universal consciousness). This involves seeking union with the universe or universal energy, not the Christian God of the Bible. This process is about connecting with the divine presence within. What it is not is a connection to Jesus.

According to the *Yoga Sutras*, yoga aims to attain a state of the "yogas citta vrtti nirodhah," which translates to "The restraint of the modifications of the mind-stuff is yoga.[3]" It goes on to say, "In this sutra, Patanjali gives the goal of Yoga… If the restraint of the mental modifications is achieved, one has reached the goal of Yoga… The entire science of Yoga is based on this.[3]" The whole purpose is to bring the mind to a state of stillness, clarity, and inner peace. The belief is that when you are in this state of mind, it allows for deeper self-realization and connection with your true self or higher consciousness. The movements in yoga are only used to help you get to the place where you are experiencing Samadi, which is considered total freedom.[1] The goal of yoga is not exercise, sweating it out, getting your heart rate pumping, becoming flexible, relaxing, or anything of the sort. The goal is spiritual, and you can't separate that from the physical aspects, even if your desire is only to lose weight, be more flexible, or de-stress.

When you practice the physical side of yoga, you are practicing stability and breathing with ease. Do you know why this is important? It's so you can learn to sit in the postures for extended amounts of time as you shift the focus inward and prepare your body for meditation. You are then supposed to work through the seven other limbs of yoga to create harmony.

This is where the relationship between karma and yoga comes in. Did you know that karma and yoga are intertwined? In

Hindu and yogic philosophy, the Law of Karma states that every action, thought, and intention has consequences. Individuals are believed to accumulate karma based on their actions, which will influence their future experiences and their life circumstances. Yoga philosophy acknowledges karma's believed impact on life and emphasizes the importance of self-awareness, intentionality, and ethical responsibility.[4] It doesn't sound that bad, right?

There actually is some truth in there. This is where I would look at the intersectionality of what I learned and what Christianity is. On the surface, your actions do have consequences, and self-awareness, intentionality, and ethical responsibility all sound so Biblical and in some ways are; the Bible clearly talks about the concept of sowing and reaping. As a Christian, the main thing is always Jesus. If we remove Him from the equation, it's humanistic thinking. If we try to merge Him into another belief system, well, that's just like mixing two different puzzle sets and trying to fit the pieces together. It just doesn't work.

The belief is that if you practice yoga with a mindful and positive attitude, you can help create positive karma and contribute to personal growth and transformation. Conversely, acting with harmful intentions or engaging in yogic practices with a sense of ego or competitiveness can generate negative karma.[4] This is why they tell you to focus on your own yoga practice in classes. They discourage you from looking around the room at others and to focus on yourself.

I've heard it said that the enemy will counterfeit the things of God. A counterfeit is something fake, it's an imitation.

Remember, the aim of yoga is liberation or freedom from the cycle of birth, death, and rebirth. Its aim is to eliminate suffering. The concept of karma in yoga was described in my training as the reason for hardships and sufferings in life. The concept was used to explain things like children born with deformities and people who inherently struggle in life vs. those who don't. As I was listening and taking notes, I realized the belief system surrounding yoga was all about "works." It is centered around a works-based belief system to eliminate suffering.

The Bible on the other hand says Salvation, which is true freedom, is a free gift and is not something earned through works, good deeds, or good karma (Ephesians 2:8-9, paraphrased). As a Christ follower we do not have to "work" to eliminate suffering. I've heard it said before that pain is inevitable but suffering is a choice, and I agree with that statement. Pain, hurt, and disappointments happen in a fallen world, even as a Christ follower. So much so that Jesus made it a point to tell His disciples in John 16:33, "...In the world you have tribulation and trials and distress and frustration; but be of good cheer [take courage; be confident, certain, undaunted]! For I have overcome the world. [I have deprived it of power to harm you and have conquered it for you]" (AMPC). Our focus is not to erase suffering from our lives. Jesus reminds us that challenges, trials, and pain will come, but the victory is already His. All we have to do is to stand firm in that promise, and in the midst of anything that tries to dim that, remember that we are not abandoned in the midst of a storm, we're guided and protected by the One who has already overcome it all.

You may be wondering, how does this all connect? Well, in my yoga teacher training I learned that when practicing yoga there is an end goal concerning karma.

1. The first aspect of this journey is to stop creating new karma.

2. The second aspect is to work through old karma.

3. The end goal of this journey is to attain a state of freedom, which is called moksha. Moksha is when you are freed from the constraints of the physical world and the cycles of birth and rebirth.

The philosophies behind the practice of yoga, as well as its connection to karma, are a counterfeit gospel. And, because the practice of yoga is inherently rooted in Hindu beliefs, the notion that divinity and goodness are within every person is also a counterfeit gospel. It suggests that one must go deep inside of themselves to draw on that which is within. The overall belief is that this is where freedom comes from, freedom from suffering. This is not what the Bible says. The Bible says in Jeremiah 17:9 that the heart is deceitful. And we know that freedom only comes through Christ, as stated in Galatians 5: "At last we have freedom, for Christ has set us free! We must always cherish this truth and firmly refuse to go back into the bondage of our past" (TPT).

In my journey through yoga teacher training, I was faced with the truth that God holds the number one spot in my life, and if there is anything competing with that spot, it must be cut off. Now this isn't the first time I've had to sever something from my life and I'm sure it won't be the last, but my prayer is each time God reveals something that must go, my response will be, "Yes, Lord."

So there you go. That's the point. Yoga has an ultimate end goal, liberation, and that has nothing to do with flexibility. The pursuit is to stop creating personal karma and work through all the old karma to reach liberation. The goal is to be free, but **true freedom is only found in Christ.**

IS THERE SUCH A THING AS CHRISTIAN YOGA?

So, what about Christian yoga? Is that a thing? After realizing yoga was a no go for me, I combed through the internet trying to find anyone that had a similar experience to mine, and part of me was also looking for a solution. I stumbled across something that seemed strange given all I just learned, Christian yoga. I was cautious but also somewhat intrigued. Now, back when I first started this journey, there weren't as many alternative yoga sites as there are now, but with the few I saw I noticed a trend: it was basically yoga repackaged with different names attached to each movement.

I eventually figured out the concept of Christian yoga is a source of debate, and it depends on who you ask; for some, the attempt to adapt and modify yoga practices to align with Christian beliefs and values is done to redeem the yoga practice. Some Christians find it compatible to practice yoga and Christianity with no sense of dissonance. Then there are those like myself, who view it as contradictory or conflicting with Christianity. However, I can say that I do understand, to a certain extent, because I, too, was in a place of wanting to take yoga and rebrand it, which is what every other person who has culturally appropriated the practice has done.

Christian yoga is an oxymoron.

But, here's the thing, the fundamental elements of yoga are Hindu, and that is the thing that grieves my spirit. Yoga involves references to Hindu deities, spiritual concepts, and practices that do not align with Biblical teaching. Yoga classes labeled as "Christian yoga" may incorporate Biblical references, Christian prayers, and other things that may feel relatable to a Christ follower, but Christian yoga is an oxymoron.

As stated, I didn't always believe Christian yoga was an oxymoron. I've said and thought things such as: "I'm only here for the exercise, not the spiritual side of yoga; when everyone meditates, I meditate on the Word." When everyone would say, "OM," (which the *Yoga Sutras* describes as a mystic sound that represents gods name as well as form)[1], I would pray. In my previous way of thinking, I used the physical movements and breathing techniques for health, relaxation, and as a means to connect with God. This mindset was my overall approach when something happened that grieved my spirit. I would pray or say the name of Jesus to combat what was happening inside so I could keep on with class, and continue practicing. Compromise. If practicing yoga naturally aligned with Christian beliefs and values, we as Christians wouldn't have to make so many accommodations in order to participate. There would not be a need to omit saying "OM," pray while they meditate, dismiss what's being said during class, or say "Jesus" while the rest of the class chants. I want to share that in those moments I never knew what "OM" meant, but I knew in my spirit it wasn't something I should be saying.

Yoga is yoga. We don't get to tell yoga what yoga is. We can't just rebrand another belief system and slap the word "Christian" in front of it. At the most basic level, Hinduism and Christianity are just different. They have their own set of beliefs, practices, and worldviews. It is not appropriate to rebrand Hinduism as "Christian Hinduism" or take the "parts" of Hinduism that are likeable and merge them with Christianity. None of this is Biblical.

There are many young women, and men, who seem to genuinely love the Lord and feel they have found their calling who have chosen to teach yoga from a Christian perspective. So many, in fact, that there is a whole "Christian Yoga" following. There are so many believers who practice yoga, and either have a desire to put a Christian spin on it or have already put a spin on it, that there's a whole association that governs the movement. I get it. Again, there was a time where I thought I would do it as well.

I have spoken to and followed the accounts of several Christian women who believe in the practice of yoga, and the main idea stems from a place of wanting to use yoga to help people draw closer to God. This is a common phrase used by many, and it's easy to acquiesce to a statement like that because who wants to say to someone, *God didn't call you to that*. Until one day, I realized the obvious, and that is that God already took care of how we draw close to Him. He already provided a way for us to draw near to Him. He gave His only Son so that we could be reconciled to Him, and opened the door for us to live in daily communion with Him. We don't need yoga as the bridge. I know, I know, no one is saying that yoga replaces Jesus, but to allude to the notion that engaging in another spiritual practice

> Yoga is yoga. We don't get to tell yoga what yoga is.

outside of Christianity will help you grow closer to God is foolish.

This idea of Christian yoga is not a new thing; it actually started back in the late twentieth century, and the outcome of that movement has a school called, The School of the Natural Order. The school's logo is a serpent coiled around the neck of an eagle. They say the serpent represents wisdom, and its spiral form represents, you guessed it, the Kundalini. Guess what another name for this is? The "christos." They refer to this serpent energy as the "christos." This has been the school's logo since its inception in the 1920s. As outlined on their site, the logo represents "the eagle ('spiritual' vision) carrying the serpent (christos power) to 'great heights', the ascent of the force to the crown center.[3]" This is the language used by the school that the creator of Christian yoga founded.

People can choose to believe what they want, they can be educated where they wish, and they can worship who they want, but when I read this, my discernment kicked up a notch. This does not align with Biblical teaching, yet it's a school birthed out of the Christian yoga movement.

The whole foundation of Christian yoga is built on Antichrist symbolism and anti-Biblical teaching. Jesus said you should worship the Lord your God and serve Him only (Luke 4:8 NKJV, paraphrased). The Bible emphasizes the exclusive worship of the one true God and warns against engaging in activities or practices that connect to other gods or idols. Christians are called to remain faithful to God and to avoid any form of idolatry or spiritual compromise.

Some still emphasize the compatibility of yoga with Christianity and promote the idea that yoga can be practiced as a form of worship, prayer, and meditation that can deepen your relationship with God, but that's the total opposite of everything the Bible teaches. Some emphasize another rebuttal, expressing their desire is to redeem Yoga. I don't agree with this either. You can't redeem another religion, faith, or philosophy. That's like saying I'm going to practice some other religion, but instead of praying to their god, I'm going to pray to the God of the Bible. How does that work? It doesn't. It's a deception. To try to "Christianize" yoga is like mixing oil and water; no matter how much you stir, they don't blend because their very natures are incompatible.

I do want to highlight that I am not against the idea of redeeming things for the Kingdom of God. There are indeed things in this world that can be redeemed. Let's consider the rainbow. In today's culture, it has been adopted by various non-faith-based movements, but we know it's true origin comes from God. The rainbow was given as a symbol of His promise to Noah after the flood, a sign of His faithfulness and His covenant with creation. The rainbow can be reclaimed because its original meaning is authored by the God of the Bible.

What about something that is less obvious? Let's say a pumpkin. Pumpkins can be used in unholy practices, but the vegetable itself is neutral; it belongs to God's creation, the pumpkin itself wasn't created for evil.

However, yoga is not like the rainbow or the pumpkin. It wasn't created by the God of the Bible, and yoga at its core is not a neutral practice. It wasn't created with God's truth in mind; rather, it is deeply tied to a spiritual belief system that is incompatible with Christianity. Its origins are rooted in practices meant to connect with spiritual energies, attain enlightenment, and focus on self-realization. None of those things align with the message of the Gospel. Yoga is not just exercise. You cannot separate the movements from the practice of yoga, no matter how bad someone may want to try and make it work.

How do you redeem something that is fundamentally at odds with Christianity? When attempting to redeem or merge yoga with Christianity, it reveals the underlying incompatibility. The teachings of yoga are just different. Yoga carries spiritual implications that conflict with Biblical teachings. As Christians, we are called to rely on Christ alone.

Go on a little allegorical journey with me:

Imagine yourself as a gardener. Your faith is your garden. It's a lush garden filled with diverse and beautiful plants. This garden of faith is where you connect with God. It's where intimacy is attained. You diligently work day and night watering the soil, pruning, and carefully tending to the needs of each plant to ensure they are healthy and thriving.

You are gifted a "yoga plant," and it's beautiful to the senses: the look, the smell, the colors. You're excited; it's a plant unlike any you've ever seen before. It's unique. The only caveat is that it comes with its own soil. You see no issues, and you immediately introduce this "yoga plant" to your garden without considering the consequences or conducting research because excitement does that sometimes.

Your new plant is now integrated into your faith garden, and you learn over time that this "yoga plant" brings an invasive root system. You realize that the roots will begin to grow in such a way that they will intertwine with the other plants. And the soil the plant came with contains elements inconsistent with the already nutrient-rich soil of the garden you have so lovingly cared for.

This gift that you were once so excited about will eventually lead to chaos, and the delicate balance of your garden's ecosystem will be disrupted. You now know that this gift carries unintended consequences.

Do you immediately remove the plant and decontaminate the soil? Or do you wait and see what happens, thinking you can somehow manage the chaos as the yoga roots begin to intertwine with the other plants and the nutrient-dense soil becomes contaminated?

Does it matter that you, the gardener, didn't know this would happen? That your intentions were different?

Practicing yoga is like introducing a foreign plant and its soil into a Spirit-filled garden. This is why discernment is so important. What we allow into our garden is vital.

The Lure Of Deception

It was drilled into my head that yoga is not a religion, but when I purchased all my yoga books, they were in the religion section of a very well-known bookstore. I'm not sure if this has changed in recent years, but it was certainly true then. Yoga has made a name for itself here in the West, and according to Yogi Times, as of February 2025, "300 + million" people practice yoga globally, with about 36.7 million Americans practicing regularly.[4] I often wonder how many of those Americans are Spirit-filled, Bible-believing Christians who love the Lord and would be appalled to learn that what they are engaging in is not "just exercising" but inherently religious, particularly within the context of Hindu worship.

I wonder if, after sharing my yoga teacher training story, there are readers thinking, *Okay, well, that's your personal experience, but that's not my experience with yoga, so how does all this apply to me?* Well, that's a great question, so I'm going to attempt to answer it.

One of the most important things I did when sorting through this yoga dilemma was get into the Word. I went straight to the Old Testament to see if yoga was discussed in any way, shape, or form. That way, I had proof directly from the source, and I wasn't talking about my own subjective experience. I want to share what I found with you.

Okay, let's turn to Genesis, the first book of the Bible where we will find God's initial plan for mankind. Here is where God outlines the way things were supposed to be before the fall, and this is also where we'll find, drum roll, absolutely nothing about yoga.

The Bible never says, "Don't practice yoga," but the Bible also never says, "Don't run through a minefield." Just because the Bible never explicitly says, "Don't practice yoga," doesn't mean that leaping into it without questioning, researching, or heeding the warnings of those who have experienced its effects is not warranted. I didn't do any of that and practiced for years. It wasn't until yoga teacher training that I learned exactly what yoga really was. So, while I wasn't able to find a direct reference to yoga in the Word, I was able to find what the Word says in relation to the many warnings scattered throughout Scripture that speak to the broader aspects of practicing yoga.

The reality, albeit a difficult discussion, is that the lure of deception is highly subtle, so much so that when someone is deceived, they are unaware they're being deceived. I didn't realize this until I was sitting in the middle of a circle with other lovely people talking about Atman and Brahman, serpent energy, and reincarnation. I didn't believe any of these things, but I was in a class to learn about it with the intention of teaching others. When a person is in a deceptive state, they will fight tooth and nail for the framework they believe in. Others around them can see it, but they themselves don't realize it. I know this because if anyone were to ask me about yoga back then, I would have made it fit my Christian framework.

We are called to worship the God of Genesis 1:1 who created the universe, not the universe itself, not energy, not stars, and not the moon or the sun. Even though I never worshiped any of these things inside or outside the context of yoga, I would steer very clear of any teachings that do not align with the Word of God, and I would refrain from engaging in practices that incorporate any spirituality contrary to the teachings outlined in the 66 books of the Bible. Anything less can and will eventually open the door to give the enemy a foothold.

Deception is sneaky, sneaky. By adding a dash or two of truth, deception creates a space where you initially latch onto the truth until the rest of the ingredients seep their way into your being. I know for a fact that if the first yoga class I ever attended was blatantly up front about the true meaning of the practice, I would have acknowledged exactly what was happening. But, I didn't get that. The job of deception is to blur the line between the truth and a lie, making it hard to detect. What I did learn is that I can't afford to let my spiritual guard down. Deception is like someone who creates counterfeits and uses just enough details to make the item or experience look or seem real. Deception seems like the real deal, that's the purpose, this is why everything must be measured against the teachings of Scripture. Gone are the days of just accepting ideas, philosophies, and practices into our lives without questioning the spiritual implications. This is why it's so important to be grounded in God's Word, allowing it to illuminate any shadowy areas of our thinking, feelings, and actions.

In 2 Corinthians 6:14, we are told not to be unequally yoked with unbelievers, and even though this verse refers to relationships, its meaning can easily extend to the practices we engage in. I'm not saying you shouldn't be around those that don't believe the same things as you; if that were the case, I'd be alone in this world. I'm talking about not yoking to things that are unBiblical, and yoga literally means "to yoke." Consequently, by participating in yoga, a yoke is taking place.

In the atmosphere of yoga classes, there's more than just mats and eager patrons ready to participate in class; in addition to the unseen spiritual realm, there are ideas, principles, and philosophies shared, and unintended or not, the instructor's words will be subconsciously added to the mental framework of the people taking the class. The saying "Birds of a feather flock together" can mean that people with similar traits naturally gravitate toward each other, but when you think about it with 1 Corinthians 15:33-34 in mind, it hits a little different. It then becomes, "Birds of feather flock together, not because they are the same, but because they will become the same." The phrase goes from shared traits drawing people together to the ways we continually shape each other. Now, I'm not saying that there can't be beauty in relationships built in these settings, but I am saying the beauty of relationships is in their transformative power. If you're the one being transformed and not doing any transforming, then it may be time to reevaluate some things.

This isn't about judgment but about protecting your spirit. For me, I had to make the decision to walk away because yoga is designed to change your mindset into one that aligns with the principles and philosophies of yoga. If you aren't careful, that is not a hard transformation because not all of yoga's principles and philosophies are in opposition to the things of God; some of it is good, and I found myself agreeing with the philosophies that aligned more with my belief system, mainly the ethical stuff.

For example, the ethical aspects of yoga, the yamas and niyamas, emphasize the belief that practicing yoga can nurture moral values such as compassion, kindness, and love.[5] They are defined as, "...foundational to all yogic thought." Stating that, "Yoga is a sophisticated system that extends far beyond doing yoga postures; it is literally a way of living.[5]" The yamas are non-violence, truthfulness, no stealing, non-excess, and non-possessiveness, and the niyamas are purity, contentment, self-discipline, self-study, and surrender.[5] As a Christ follower, it was easy to say yes to this kind of thing, but on the flipside, it was easy to say no to the word "namaste." Once I learned what namaste meant, that was always a source of contention for me.

According to *Merriam-Webster*, "namaste" is a picture of the religious and secular coming together (their words, not mine). They continue on to say that namaste is a word associated with both Hinduism and yoga and originates from Sanskrit. It literally means "bowing to you" or "I bow to you" and is used as a greeting.[6] In the majority of my yoga classes, the instructor would start and end the class with the term. I was taught that it meant, "The divine in me honors the divine in you," or "The divine in me bows to the divine in you." It is meant as a point of connection. The greeting says that we are all equal, I acknowledge you, you acknowledge me, and there is a shared sense of gratitude in that. On the surface, it sounds kind, respectful, and some would say beautiful, but I could never get behind saying it. I remember saying it a handful of times after a Christian friend that practiced yoga gave me a different way to think about it. Nevertheless, I always felt convicted if I did say it and eventually stopped altogether. I settled on the Biblical truth that the divine light inside me is not the universe or an energy, but Jesus: the Jesus through Whom everything was created, including the universe, and Who bows down to no one. The Bible says in Philippians 2:10-11 that at the name of Jesus, every knee should bow, in heaven and on earth and under the earth (ESV), so if someone said "namaste" to me, I didn't stop them, I just never said it back.

Is it dangerous to practice yoga just for exercise? Well, if I invited you to move bricks for arm strength, and then you found out you were helping build a satanic altar, would you stay just because you were building arm strength and toning your biceps? Once I learned there was no separation between what yoga truly is and the exercise benefit, it became a – not today, not tomorrow, not ever for me. If you struggle in this area, try not to focus on just the physical aspects of yoga, but look at it as a whole. It will be a gamechanger. The benefits do not always justify the means.

PART TWO:

Mind + Body + Spirit; God's Way

CLOSE OPEN DOORS

Many people have the same thoughts: *Isn't yoga just a bunch of stretching exercises? It's not a religion. Isn't it just a trendy workout? Who cares about its origins or cultural context?* Aside from the sheer cultural appropriation, as a Christian, it's more important to be mindful when incorporating practices from different cultures, especially when it comes to practices that have a spiritual or religious component that contradict the Bible in any way.

This sort of statement can be triggering for some, especially when we live in a society that is inundated with things that originate from different forms of paganism. Sometimes it's just hard to know what sayings, customs, celebrations, art, etc. derives from ancient pagan rituals or ways of life. There are the blatant ones, and then there are many still shrouded in mystery or ignorance. This is why our relationship with God and pursuing knowledge, wisdom, understanding, and discernment is so important. Allow His Holy Spirit to speak to you, lead you, and guide you. We are reminded in Ephesians our fight is not against flesh and blood, but against principalities, powers, and against the rulers of the darkness of this world (Ephesians 6:12 NKJV, paraphrased). If you've said yes to Jesus, you've signed up for a war, whether you realize it or not. If you don't acknowledge the fight, that's okay, but the war doesn't stop. There are powers in place that seek to weaken you and separate you from walking in relationship with God. Keeping your eyes open and being spiritually alert is part of walking the Christian walk.

Let's talk about open doors. It's so important to recognize the power we hold in our choices. We open doors to the enemy when we step outside the safe refuge of God's guidance; He warns us against giving the enemy a foothold in Ephesians chapter four.

Engaging in spiritual practices that do not align with the Word of God is like giving the enemy a big fat invitation into your life. As believers, we are meant to be enveloped in God's protection, but if we step outside of that, knowingly or unknowingly, we put ourselves at risk. Psalm 91 emphasizes this: "He who dwells in the secret place of the Most High shall abide under the shadow of the Almighty. I will say of the Lord, "*He* is my refuge and my fortress; my God, in Him I will trust." Surely He shall deliver you from the snare of the fowler *and* from the perilous pestilence. He shall cover you with His feathers, and under His wings you shall take refuge;..."

I've heard many stories of well-meaning women who began with practicing yoga to stretch their body and, over time, found themselves drawn deeper into the new age. Stretching may open the body but yoga opens a door. I thank God that I never ventured too deep into areas that drew me away from Him or dulled my senses to hearing His voice, but I do remember being curious and researching certain things that seemed interesting at the time, things I never would have engaged with otherwise.

One thing that stands out to me is sage. The use of sage isn't unusual in the yoga community, and at first, it didn't seem strange to me because I grew up in a house where we burned incense, mainly for the smell. But after learning more about what sage was and why someone would use it, I decided it wasn't something I wanted to be involved with. If I hadn't been in a community where people used sage, I may have never felt the desire to research it or try it. The enemy works in subtle ways, trying to lure us into spaces where we start dabbling with things that can leave us vulnerable to his influence and plans. Solomon's wisdom sheds a bright light on this topic: "Can a man take fire in his bosom, and his clothes not be burned?" (Proverbs 6:27 NKJV).

The concept of open doors in a Christian's life is a serious one that should not be taken lightly. Ephesians 4:27 conveys that we can give the devil a foothold in our lives. The amplified version says do not give the devil an opportunity. This implies that we can leave room or give opportunities for the devil to gain access into our lives. We are supposed to be alert, observing what's happening not only in us but around us. We don't want to ignore the red flags that God waves in front of us, using our own justifications rather than God's wisdom. And, it is so easy to justify things in this world. When you really want something, it's easy to make it sound right. Looking back over my journey, I justified so many things and bypassed that feeling and nudge to not take yoga classes, and I replaced it with my own rationale.

Think back over your life, and pick out some times when you found yourself ignoring what you now know was the Holy Spirit prompting you to walk away, say no, or say yes, and you did the opposite. Now that you're on the other side, you're able to look back and see the big picture. You can clearly see the repercussions of the choices you made and the grace of God over your life in those areas. You have information now that you didn't have then because you now know the outcome. For some, you may have even contemplated, "What would things be like if I had listened then?" The wonderful thing is that we serve a redeeming God, and He can and does step into the things we've created a mess of to redeem those areas, but if you don't learn from those experiences, it's easy to find yourself in the same spot again under different circumstances. This is why being mindful of when the enemy is trying to gain a foothold in your life is so important so you don't end up in the same cycles over and over again. Be mindful of the doors you open. Listen to the Holy Spirit's prompting, and walk in obedience. As not only professing Christians but as Christians who have a desire to live out the Word of God; may we always keep our eyes fixed on Jesus, who is the Way, the TRUTH, and the Life (John 14:4

NKJV, paraphrased). God will shed the light of truth on any situation if you remain in Him.

I still remember those not-so-subtle pricks I felt in my spirit during certain yoga classes I was in. It was an uncomfortable, "I don't belong in this space" feeling. It would usually happen at the beginning of class when the instructor guided everyone to set an intention for the class or participate in a guided meditation. Sometimes it would happen at the end of class when the instructor would prompt everyone into Shavasana, or dead man's pose, which is laying on your back, palms up, feet falling out to the side – like a dead man. These are the moments when I would pray in my head, say the name of Jesus, or recite whatever Scripture came to mind to "cover" myself. Depending on the instructor, we were sometimes prompted to recite something while in this pose. I didn't say a thing, I would just be quiet and focus on Jesus. In my mind, I would think, I'm not here for all that; I only wanted to exercise.

> You shouldn't have to feel like you need to cover yourself, place a hedge of protection around yourself, or focus on the name of Jesus to exercise...

The main question is, why should I have had to do all that if yoga is just an exercise class? I've never been to a gym and felt convicted that I shouldn't use a particular machine, or I've never been to a fitness class and felt the need to place a hedge of protection around myself because we were doing squats. You shouldn't have to feel like you need to cover yourself, place a hedge of protection around yourself, or focus on the name of Jesus to exercise, unless you accidentally signed up for some sort of extreme fitness program. Then good luck. In my case, the concept of having to do all that should have been a row of red flags flapping in the wind and creating a sound so loud that I couldn't even focus on anything else. I know now that connecting with God during class wasn't only out of a desire to connect with Him as a distraction from what was happening around me: for me, it was a need because without His presence, I felt exposed to things in the spirit that made me feel off. Why do I share this? Because it's moments like this, that, if overlooked, can cause other things to seem acceptable, and you can find yourself drifting from God and the sound of His voice.

How Do You Know When A Door Has Been Opened In Your Life?

An open door has happened when you find yourself easily tolerating things you wouldn't usually tolerate. Many people who practice yoga often find themselves incorporating or exploring various aspects of New Age philosophy alongside their yoga routines. For those of us that are Christian, this is not something that's usually sought out; it's more of a natural progression of being around the New Age and beginning to feel comfortable in that environment. Being immersed in the New Age environment can lead to a growing comfort with its lifestyle, prompting reflection and exploration that may not have seemed appealing at first. Especially if there is no guard up. 1 Corinthians 15:33 says, "Do not be misled, bad company corrupts good character". Now, I'm not talking about being in an environment with purpose. There are ministries that do the amazing work of going into dark places to bring the Gospel. But they're not partaking in what's happening; they are on a mission to bring the light of Christ into the darkness. I am addressing Christians that are in spaces where they are sitting under the teaching of New Age thinking and philosophies consuming what's being shared. They are trying to take "the good" and leave out "the bad." The result is tolerance, acceptance, and eventually incorporating things into their lives that are anti-Biblical.

For example, as a Bible-believing, Spirit-filled Christian, if someone approached you and asked if you believed in chakras, let alone if they could help you align your chakras, you would probably say no. Beliefs about chakras are interconnected with concepts of reincarnation and karma, and interwoven throughout yoga philosophy. Karma is where the soul undergoes birth, death, and rebirth cycles based on past actions. These concepts are not part of the Christian belief system. Christianity teaches that each person lives one life, and that life must be reconciled to God through Jesus to experience eternal life. In a yoga class, it is not uncommon to focus on opening the heart chakra because yoga, meditation, and energy healing are used to open, balance, and align the chakra to promote overall health and vitality. Sitting in a class that guides you through these open doors is how Christians find themselves caught in a spiral of unfamiliar behaviors, gradually shifting their core beliefs and straying from their intended path.

The Word of God warns us, "See to it that no one takes you captive through hollow and deceptive philosophies, which depends on human tradition and the elemental spiritual forces of this world rather than on Christ" (Colossians 2:8). If not acknowledged, allowing yourself to be led through these kinds of activities can lead to a slow straying away from the principles of Christ. Even I eventually found myself engaging in actions I never imagined I would. What felt like just going with the flow of class meant tolerating things I thought were no big deal and, worse, at times putting my Christian spin on them. Looking back, this way of thinking could have easily led me away from Biblical truths and into practicing things I never envisioned engaging in. It was, at the core, watering down the truth and justifying it.

New Age Practices That Often Accompany The Yogic Lifestyle

I want to share a list of New Age practices, most that are not uncommon to see practiced alongside yoga. As I reflected on the practices that seemed common, both among those who practice yoga and even those who don't but have adopted the trends of today's culture, I felt led to dig even deeper into the New Age movement. What I found was eye-opening, evident when looked at through a Biblical lens, but eye-opening nonetheless. All of these practices are spiritually dangerous, and there are clear Biblical reasons for avoiding each one. If you have engaged in any of these practices either through lifestyle or curiosity, there is no condemnation for those in Christ Jesus. There is freedom in forgiveness through repentance.

This list is not exhaustive, but serves as a starting point of things to be mindful of:

Angel Cards[1]

These are cards used for spiritual guidance. "Demons disguise themselves as angels, and can give amazingly accurate predictions which tangle you up in a satanic web of deceit. The demons will give you a mixture of truth and lies, to hook you in and lead you to deception."

Angel Numbers/Numerology[1,2]

Before we talk about angel numbers and numerology, I would like to highlight the fact that, since the Bible was originally written in Hebrew, numerical symbolism has been woven throughout the Word of God. In Hebrew, there are 22 letters, and each letter has a numerical value. Nothing is done by accident; there is purpose in everything God does, and this is just another way that He brings Proverbs 25:2 to life.

Numerology on the other hand is a belief system that looks at the significance of numbers and their influence on our lives, likewise the concept behind angel numbers is rooted in numerology. In angel numbers, each number is associated with certain vibrations and meanings. People who follow this belief often pay attention to these sequences as a way to gain insight into their life and use it to make decisions or find reassurance. God wants us to seek Him for all answers.

Astral Projection[3]

Astral projection, also known as astral travel, astral plane, or soul travel, is described as a practice where a person believes they can learn to voluntarily separate their astral, non-material self from their body and travel to other physical locations or possibly to an astral realm through meditation.

Astrology/Horoscopes/Zodiac Signs[1,4]

Astrology is defined as, "the divination of the supposed influences of the stars and planets on human affairs and terrestrial events by their positions and aspects." Horoscopes fall under this umbrella and are used to make predictions based on people's zodiac signs from astrology. The concept of zodiac signs are that when you were born, the stars and planets were in special spots, and some people believe those spots have the ability to give insight into a person's life or affairs. Some people use astrology for fun, and others for meaning. Some people think this helps them understand themselves better, their friends better, and even who they should connect with or not connect with in their intimate relationships. Identifying people's birthdays as seasons with their astrological signs has also become common. You may hear people, even Christians, say, "It's Aquarius season." This is not a fun or lighthearted trend. "The royal astrologers of Babylon were humbled when they stood next to Daniel." In Daniel 1:20, he was found to have greater wisdom and insight than all the magicians and enchanters in the king's court; and when it came to interpreting the king's dream it says, the astrologers were powerless, while Daniel, lead by God, revealed both the dream and its meaning (Daniel 2:27, paraphrased).

"Astrology as a form of divination is expressly forbidden in Scripture (Deuteronomy 18:10-14)." Astrology and horoscopes are used as an attempt to figure out one's destiny due to a lack of direction, but our eyes are meant to stay fixed on the Lord. He authors our destiny.

Chakras

Chakras are considered energy centers in the body that correlate to specific colors. They are thought to influence physical, emotional, and spiritual well-being. It is believed that when these energy centers are balanced, individuals may experience a sense of harmony and well-being. Conversely, blockages or imbalances in the chakras can lead to various physical or emotional issues, prompting some people to explore practices like meditation, yoga, or energy work to restore balance.

Christ Consciousness[1]

"Christ consciousness claims a belief in Jesus Christ, but it actually promotes faith in one's own ability to make oneself pleasing to God through attitude changes and mystical experiences. 1 John 4:1 gives us direction concerning philosophies such as Christ consciousness: "Do not believe every spirit, but test the spirits to see whether they are from God, because many false prophets have gone out into the world." The consciousness that pleases Christ is for human beings to recognize that we are sinners (Romans 3:23), confess Jesus as Savior and Lord (Romans 10:8–9), and love Him with all our heart, soul, mind, and strength and our neighbor as ourselves (Luke 10:27)."

Crystal Healing[1]

Crystal healing is a practice that involves using crystals or gemstones for physical, emotional, or spiritual healing. The idea is that different crystals possess specific energies or vibrations that can interact with the human body's energy to restore balance and promote well-being. On the surface this is not entirely false, because yes, crystals, flowers, plants, rocks, etc. all vibrate at a certain frequency, and yes, God created our bodies with energy pathways; but God instructs us to put our faith in Him, not taking crystals for use in energy work or spell casting. "While the Bible is filled with references to crystals, nowhere are we told to worship them or use them as a substitute for going directly to God." When you put your faith in God's creation rather than in Him as the Creator, you are out of alignment. True healing comes from the Lord alone, not through divination or witchcraft. Jeremiah 17:14 (AMP) says, "Heal me, O Lord, and I will be healed; save me, and I will be saved, for You are my praise." It's only in Him we find healing and restoration. Can and does the Lord use natural means to heal? Yes, but He never goes against His Word, and seeking the New Age for healing is not Biblical.

Dream Catchers[1]

"The purpose of a dream catcher is to catch dreams—that is, to trap bad or evil dreams and channel good dreams to the sleeper. New age borrows from many different cultures without realizing the underlying meaning or implications. Dream catchers are usually placed in a window or above the bed, allowing the good dreams to drip down the feathers onto the sleeper below."

Enneagram[5,6,7,8]

To me, the others seem obvious, but this one was a shock to me. I had to do some digging to find out what the Enneagram really was because I was on the bandwagon with this one. Enneagram is another one that is not directly tied to a lifestyle of yoga but it is popular, therefore I wanted to share what I found.

So, what is the Enneagram exactly? It's a system that describes nine distinct personality types. Many people use this today as a fun way to understand their personality. If you haven't taken the test yourself, I'm sure you know someone who has referred to themselves as a 6 or a 7 on the diagram. The Enneagram, like yoga, is rooted in New Age philosophy; it's not Biblical, and it can create open doors in your life.

I want to share a brief history of its origins to help you understand the why. Oscar Ichazo was a Bolivian philosopher and is known for developing the Enneagram of Personality. He also founded the Arica School in the 1970s, which is heavily laden with New Age philosophies. Without going too deep into the history of Ichazo, I'd like to shift to one of his students,

Claudio Naranjo, who is known for the Enneagram as it is used today. In an interview done with Eleonora Gilbert entitled "Healing Civilization," posted on Youtube in December 2010, Claudio was introduced as a central figure in the New Age movement of the 60s and 70s, an experimenter of Shamanism Sufism and Buddhism, and founder of a group in California called SAT (Seekers After Truth). Claudio acknowledged Eleonora's introduction, stating, "That describes me." He went on to say, "During the recent years, I feel I'm working more, intending to change society than people individually."

He shared the origins of the specific information about the enneatypes, saying, "It came to me through automatic writing, which I verified through observation." Now, this is where I felt a huge Las Vegas neon arrow sign pointing to get my attention. What is automatic writing? I had to look it up. Automatic writing is produced by spiritualism or any subconscious agency rather than by being conscious or aware. In spiritualism, automatic writing is when a person writes without consciously thinking about it. This usually happens when they're focused on something else, like during a séance or in a trance-like state. It's believed that in these moments, the person might channel messages from spirits or their subconscious mind, leading to writings that are involuntary. Not Biblical. Not at all.

Evil Eye[1]

The evil eye symbol is showing up everywhere nowadays, on clothes, in souvenir shops, in art. The evil eye is an ancient amulet believed to protect against negative energy or harm caused by someone else's jealousy or malice. It usually looks like a blue and white eye, and people think it can ward off bad vibes or ill wishes directed at them. Again, not Biblical.

Grand Rising[9]

Grand rising is a phrase used as an alternative to saying "good morning," but it also has a much deeper spiritual meaning. It is not really used in connection with yoga specifically, but has gained popularity in the black community, so I thought I'd throw it in for information's sake. It is believed by some spiritual communities that the spirit leaves the body and travels while asleep. When someone says, "Grandrising," they are giving thanks because their spirit has returned to their body, and they have risen once again. This is a belief system and saying that does not align with Biblical teachings.

Hypnosis[1]

Hypnosis leads to an altered state of consciousness in which the mind is very susceptible to outside suggestion. That susceptibility is what the hypnotist needs in order to modify the behavior of his subject. However, the word susceptible should concern us. Scripture says to be watchful and "self-controlled and alert."

Karma[1]

Karma is a concept that is present in both Hinduism and yoga philosophy. Yoga views karma as the law of cause and effect where every action has consequences. It recognizes that individuals create their own reality through their thoughts, choices, and actions, and these actions have repercussions on the person's physical, mental, and spiritual well-being. Galatians 6:7-8 (NASB) reads: "Do not be deceived, God is not mocked; for whatever a person sows, this he will also reap. For the one who sows to his own flesh will reap destruction from the flesh, but the one who sows to the Spirit will reap eternal life from the Spirit." Actions have consequences; that is clear in God's Word, but the difference is that consequences are tied to God's law and His judgment rather than a predetermined karmic cycle of cause and effect.

Manifesting[1]

This is one of those things that can get caught up in semantics. Webster defines manifesting as "to make evident or certain by showing or displaying." In the New Age movement, "manifesting" means believing that you can make things happen in your life by thinking positively and focusing on what you want. It's like believing that if you imagine something enough and really want it, the universe will make it happen for you. This idea comes from the belief that the universe works like a magnet, attracting things that are similar to each other. So, by thinking positively and visualizing your desires, you can attract those things into your life. On the surface, this is not entirely false because the Bible talks about the power of our thoughts and our words alike, but the major difference is aligning one's heart and will with God's purposes and trusting in His wisdom and timing. The emphasis is on surrendering to God's sovereignty and seeking

His guidance through Jesus Christ rather than attempting to manipulate reality through your individual thoughts or desires.

In James 4:3 (AMP) it says, "You ask [God for something] and do not receive, because you ask with wrong motives [out of selfishness or with an unrighteous agenda]." This is why the idea that individuals can create their own reality through focused thoughts and desires raises important concerns from a Biblical perspective. It is important to seek God's will rather than pursuing personal desires. Now, I'm not saying it's wrong to have desires, goals, dreams, hopes, vision, and such. There is nothing wrong with wanting a nice car or going on a dream vacation, but trying to attain those things through striving, thinking really hard about it, or giving it energy removes God from the equation and makes it about you and your works. Proverbs 19:21 reminds us, "Many plans are in a man's heart, but it is the Lord's purpose that prevails". This verse emphasizes a fundamental truth: it's God's purpose and plan that guides our lives, not our intentions or wishes. By recognizing this, we cultivate a deeper reliance on God, and we trust Him, not ourselves.

Psychics/Palm Reading/Tarot Card Reading/Mediums[1]

Psychic beliefs, palm readings, and tarot card readings are all practices that fall under the broader umbrella of divination, which is the art of seeking knowledge about the future or gaining insight into personal situations. Mediums are individuals who claim to have the ability to communicate with spirits or the deceased. All of these practices come from demonic sources.

In my yoga teacher training, we were taught that you can

enhance intuition and psychic abilities. This kind of thing doesn't usually come up in a regular class, but it's a part of their belief system. Deuteronomy 18:10-12 (AMP) reads: "There shall not be found among you anyone who makes his son or his daughter pass through the fire [as a sacrifice], one who uses divination and fortune-telling, one who practices witchcraft, or one who interprets omens, or a sorcerer, or one who casts a charm or spell, or a medium, or a spiritist, or a necromancer [who seeks the dead]. For whoever does these things is utterly repulsive to the Lord; and because of these detestable practices the Lord your God is driving them out before you."

Reiki and Energy Healing[1]

Reiki is a form of energy healing that involves channeling the same universal life force energy found in New Age and yoga philosophy through a person's hands to promote healing and relaxation. In yoga philosophy, the concept of prana, or life force energy, is a central component, and practicing pranayama, which is breath control, aims to balance and enhance the flow of prana in the body. This is why it is so common for those that embrace Reiki to complement with yoga and vice versa. They have similar principles of energy balancing. Reiki is also very common in massage therapy work. Whenever I'm looking for a massage therapist, I try to do as much homework as I can before scheduling. I will read their bio, look at their pictures, and pay attention to their certifications. If there's nothing glaring on their website, I just ask when I call. It is important to do your research and choose someone accordingly.

1 Thessalonians 5:22 (AMP) says, "Abstain from every form of evil [withdraw and keep away from it]." Avoid any practices perceived as evil or contrary to your Christian faith. This is why spiritual discernment is so important. Things don't always seem to have an Antichrist agenda, but they remain dangerous nonetheless. Reiki, much like physics and tarot card readings, has a source they draw from, and it's not Jesus. I know someone that practices Reiki, and I'll never forget the time she told me that everyone shows up in the room when she is drawing on energy, including the ancestors.

Reincarnation

Reincarnation is the belief that after death, a person's soul is reborn into a new body or form, experiencing multiple lifetimes in succession. In yoga, this is viewed as the soul's journey toward freedom. Hebrews 9:27 (AMP) says, "And just as it is appointed and destined for all men to die once and after this [comes certain] judgment."

Sage[1,10]

Sage is dried sagebrush which is "gathered into bundles and lit on fire for the purpose of smudging." Burning sage, or smudging, is believed to cleanse negative energy or spirits from a person, space, or object. This act is basically attributing spiritual power to something other than God. It's idolatry. Nothing in this world has the means to cleanse a person or space, or remove demons if it isn't through the name of Jesus Christ, and the power in His shed blood. In the Amplified Bible (AMP), Hebrews 9:22

says: "In fact under the Law almost everything is cleansed with blood, and without the shedding of blood there is no forgiveness [neither release from sin and its guilt]." This verse highlights the necessity of the blood of Jesus for true cleansing and forgiveness, underscoring that no other practice or object can provide the spiritual cleansing that comes from Him.

Additionally, Colossians 2:15 (AMP) says, "When He had disarmed the rulers and authorities [those supernatural forces of evil operating against us], He made a public example of them [exhibiting them as captives in His triumphal procession], having triumph over them through the cross." Jesus' already holds the victory over spiritual forces of darkness. Remember, Jesus said, "All authority (all power of rule) in heaven and on earth has been given to Me" (Matthew 28:18 AMP).

Then, in Luke 10:19, it is declared, "Behold! I have given you authority and power to trample upon serpents and scorpions, and [physical and mental strength and ability] over all the power that the enemy [possesses]; and nothing shall in any way harm you" (AMPC).

Why would you burn sage as a born-again, Bible-believing Christian when you have all the authority and power you need through Jesus to pray over your home, office, car, or any other space one would be inclined to smudge? No sage needed. Demon's don't flee because there is sage burning, they flee because of the Name above all names, Jesus! See Philippians 2:9-11, Psalm 4:8, 2 Thessalonians 3:3, and the spiritual weapons listed in Ephesians 6:10-17. The truth outlined in these verses doesn't just outshine sage, it renders it meaningless and of no value.

Superstition[11]

The definition of superstition is described as "a belief or practice resulting from ignorance, fear of the unknown, trust in magic or chance, or a false conception of causation." Superstition is usually rooted in cultural traditions and involves the idea that specific actions, events, or objects can influence luck, fate, or the outcome of particular situations. For example, when I was younger, we were not allowed to open umbrellas in the house. My friends and I never split poles when walking together. I was afraid to break a mirror. When I was very young, I never stepped on cracks while walking on the sidewalk. Why? I can tell you what somebody told me, but at the end of the day, it was all rooted in a fear of something horrible happening, and that is not the Kingdom of God. Trust God, seek His wisdom, follow Truth.

The Universe[1]

The universe is space and everything it contains. It's extremely important to note that the universe is not synonymous with God. "To a new ager, the word "Universe" is the same as "God.[1]" They are not interchangeable. God created the universe in Genesis 1; it came into being, whereas God has always been.

Close The Doors

Closing open doors to the enemy starts with asking God to reveal the open doors in your life. Think back to the list of popular new age practices you just read through. They all either openly or subtly reject Biblical truths. Have you dabbled? As Christians, it should be standard practice to examine our lives with honesty, humbling ourselves before the Lord and asking God to reveal anything we've allowed that doesn't align with His Word. Psalm 139:23-24 (AMPC) is the perfect prayer for this, "Search me [thoroughly], O God, and know my heart! Try me and know my thoughts! And see if there is any wicked or hurtful way in me, and lead me in the way everlasting." The next step being to repent, turn away from anything He reveals, confess it, and ask for His forgiveness. This next part is the best. Remember that when we confess our sins to God, the sins he already knows we are involved in, then He is faithful to forgive us of our sins and cleanse us from all unrighteousness (1 John 1:9 paraphrased).

As you embrace your freedom in Christ, make it a daily practice to submit yourselves to God. Daily submission means surrendering every part of your life to Christ, everything. Surrender your thoughts, your relationships, your mindsets, your habits, your plans, your dreams, your finances, your health, your family, your desires, everything.

Walk in the Spirit by engaging in prayer, worship, reading Scripture, and fellowship with other believers. It is also necessary to assess your living space and remove things from your home. Go through your things and ask the Holy Spirit to reveal anything that doesn't belong: trinkets, books, symbols, or any other objects in your home. It may also be necessary to step away from relationships or break unhealthy soul ties. Submit to the Lord and He will show you. Trust His process. This is not out of fear because there is no fear for those in Christ. This is about surrendering to His will for your life and closing off access points of the enemy.

PRUNING SELF-RELIANCE

How do you live in the world without being like the world? You guard yourself and root yourself in truth.

The Free Dictionary, via American Heritage Thesaurus, describes self-reliance as *"the capacity to manage one's own affairs, make one's own judgments, and provide for oneself,[1]"* emphasizing traits like independence, self-determination, and self-sufficiency.[1]

In a world that can easily lead you astray with messages that elevate self as the ultimate authority, and while culture shouts, *"Follow your heart"* and *"Do what feels right,"* the Word of God calls us to follow Christ, to deny ourselves, know God's Word, and to walk by the Spirit.

How do you live in the world without being like the world? You guard yourself and root yourself in truth. We aren't physically withdrawing from society, but rather living by a different set of values. As a person who loves community, immersing myself in the world of health and wellness has inevitably led me into spaces where I've learned to keep my eyes wide open, and to navigate these spaces with apprehension because they can be inundated with New Age practices that can lead to open doors. 1 Peter 5:8 (AMP) says, "Be sober [well balanced and self-disciplined], be alert and cautious at all times. That enemy of yours, the devil, prowls around like a roaring lion [fiercely hungry], seeking someone to devour." This has taught me to be mindful, not out of fear, but from a place of awareness. A laissez-faire approach to things isn't really my go to, especially when it comes to my faith. The Bible discusses our need for spiritual weapons in 2 Corinthians 10:3-5 for a reason. I'm not a Bible scholar, but I'd venture to say God didn't provide us with spiritual weapons just for fun; we are in a spiritual war.

The Bible says that God's power has given us everything we need for life and godliness, through our knowing the One who called us to His own glory and goodness (2 Peter 1:3 CJB). Therefore, if He provides us with everything we need to live a Godly life to include spiritual weapons of warfare, it's for a purpose. We live in a physical world, but our battle is spiritual; the enemy is actively prowling and looking for unsuspecting prey to devour. So if God provides us with spiritual weapons to defend ourselves and to guard ourselves against these attacks, I'm not going to leave them on the table. I'm going to use them.

The things of this world, including yoga, can be used as a lure. The health and wellness space is currently being used as a trap to get unsuspecting believers to embrace a barrage of various lies. This is why it's important to use discernment. New Age thinking has infiltrated these spaces and presents an ideology that seduces people into thinking they possess godlike abilities that will enrich their lives, and it's not as overt as some would think. It's wrapped in self-help philosophy that, on the surface, sounds good and sometimes relatable, but underneath, it removes the need for God from the picture and focuses on self-reliance. It teaches there is no need for God because we have the power in us. Now, I do want to be clear that as a Bible-believing, Spirit-filled follower of Christ, I believe without a shadow of doubt that there is an active, immeasurable, and unlimited power that resides in me, but it's not mine, it's God's Holy Spirit.

This concept of a godlike ability, this self-reliant and self-help mindset, is directly addressed in the Bible. Ezekiel 28:2b speaks to the proud ruler of Tyre and says, "In the pride of your heart you say, 'I am a god; I sit on the throne of a god in the heart of the seas.' But you are a mere mortal and not a god, though you think you are as wise as a god."

This verse shows a Biblical warning against equating oneself with God. On the surface it may be easy to say, "I don't do that," but our culture mirrors this ideology, and there are plenty of memes and sayings that are prevalent and have received thousands of likes and shares. These sayings may sound positive, empowering, or even harmless, but when we peel back the layers, they reflect a worldview that centers the self.

"You have all the power you need inside you."

"You are the master of your own destiny."

"You can manifest anything you want."

"The power is within you."

"Live *your* truth."

"What's true for you isn't necessarily true for me."

"Follow your heart."

"Do what feels right."

"Only *you* know what's best for you."

"Self-love is the highest form of love."

"You are enough."

"You deserve the world."

"You deserve happiness"

As followers of Christ, we understand that we are not equal to God, nor are we self-reliant.

Remember: No one succumbs to deception by believing flat-out lies. It's not always apparent. For deception to work, it sprinkles in just enough truth to disarm you, draw you in, and set the stage to make you believe it's real. That's why New Age philosophy is so dangerous, and the mindset of the world is so dangerous. The philosophy is about being your best self on the surface, but when you dig in, you realize that it completely erases the concept of Christ, the very One through whom God created everything (John 1:3 NLT).

When you believe you are the source, then you erase any need for a Savior. In a world where the enemy, the devil, prowls around like a roaring lion, seeking whom he may devour, you must be extra cautious and know what you're saying yes to (1 Peter 5:8, paraphrased). Again, this is not a fear thing; it's a discernment thing. God calls us to discern His will for our lives, always focusing on Christ and trusting Him to guide us toward what's best.

Pruning Process

Since becoming homeowners of an unexpected fixer-upper, my husband and I have learned a great deal about remodeling, renovations, and landscaping. One lesson that stands out most was regarding pruning or cutting off what doesn't belong, specifically relating to caring for the trees on our property.

For deception to work, it sprinkles in just enough truth to disarm you, draw you in, and set the stage to make you believe it's real.

We have five beautiful live oak trees on our property, and inevitably, they needed to be trimmed back not only to protect our home and its roofline, but to promote the health and growth of the trees. I did tons of research before hiring someone to visit the property for a quote. I didn't want anybody with a saw to trim our trees. I didn't want them hacked. I love trees, and I wanted a skilled arborist who knew what they were doing.

In John 15:5, Jesus tells His disciples that He is the literal energy of their lives (the vine), and they are the recipients of that energy (the branches), which bear fruit. While this verse specifically uses the metaphor of a grapevine, once I learned how trees are pruned, the Lord used our trees as a powerful visual representation of this verse and, ultimately, how God works in our lives.

I envision God as our arborist, and Jesus as the main structure of the tree (the vine), and we are the branches that grow out from that main structure and produce fruit. Any branch/es that compete with the main branch draw nutrients away from the tree, which can cause the tree to grow in the wrong direction, affecting its stability. These competing branches must be cut away. Even though they may appear healthy on the outside, what they're actually doing is causing the tree to be weakened.

Pruning trees involves carefully cutting away the excess, the unhealthy parts, and the misdirected branches. This process is what allows the tree to redirect its energy towards the most vital branches, promoting overall health, balance, and fruitfulness. If the wrong branches are cut off, the tree would slowly die. Therefore, when an arborist cares for a tree, they look for the dominant branch that provides structure and support to the whole tree (the vine), and their job is then to ensure that this main support thrives so the branches that grow out are healthy and strong.

Your spiritual life is like a tree, with Jesus as the main life-giving structure, meaning everything you need flows from Him (your strength, your guidance, your purpose, your peace, your self-control, etc.). Any excess, unhealthy, or misdirected branches that try to compete with the main branch must go. Why would you allow anything to compete with the source of your fruit?

Jesus is the One who sustains you, and without Him, no real growth or fruit can happen. That's why, when life happens, and other branches that are contrary to God's Word start to sprout, they must be cut off. This includes the belief that we as humans can be the source of our own strength, the source of our own answers, the source of our own peace, or even our own guide. We are not called to be self-reliant; we are called to rely on Him. Self-reliance is like putting a huge crown on your head and sitting on the throne of your life. This focus on inner strength and self-reliance directly competes with the Christian truth that only God sits on the throne, and that true peace and fulfillment comes from Him, not from within yourself.

Jesus is the source of everything good and life sustaining in our lives, but just like with a tree, other branches competing with that truth can begin to grow. In my situation, I had a competing belief system that appeared perfectly healthy on the surface. I had a vision to transform yoga into a Christian practice, not realizing it was simply another belief system disguised as an exercise routine. I had to learn that yoga's true objective wasn't health or fitness, but rather to gradually divert my energy and focus away from Him. It promoted self-reliance, encouraged introspection for answers, and advocated following my own heart.

I am aware that this idea of looking inside yourself for wisdom and direction is popular in today's world, but Christianity teaches something radically different. So many different belief systems, faiths, and religions encourage you to "find your truth," "listen to your inner voice," or "be your own guide." It sounds empowering, and at first glance, it seems like a harmless or even positive approach to life. But when you start to place yourself on the throne of your life, believing that the answers lie within you,

 MIND, BODY, SPIRIT - GOD'S WAY

you're essentially allowing a competing branch to grow in your heart, a branch that is trying to take the place of the one true source, Jesus.

Trust The Lord

If you've made it this far, then you already know that yoga is no exercise routine. Yoga is a spiritual practice with a physical component, and it's rooted in philosophies that do not align with Christianity. I wish I had someone to explain it so plainly to me. I received "You shouldn't practice yoga" with no reason or understanding of what made this particular type of "exercise" wrong. I'm a why person. I like to know the big picture. Sometimes it serves me well, and sometimes it takes me on journeys. For me, the thing that opened my eyes was going through yoga teacher training and learning the real deal, and that is the enemy loves open doors; it is a slow process that doesn't happen overnight. Trees don't die or fall over in a week or even a month. It takes time. To practice yoga as a Christian, even if your intent is only for physical exercise, you are nurturing a competing branch. You are feeding another truth other than the truth of God. It's dangerous territory when the focus shifts from God's wisdom to another belief or philosophy.

To grow and bear the fruit God desires in your life, the competing branch of yoga or any other belief system, mindset, or idol must be pruned. To thrive spiritually, everything that competes with Jesus must go. Yoga is subtle yet pervasive. It must be removed.

For me, the pruning away of yoga wasn't easy. I enjoyed it. It was a part of my routine, I saw and felt the benefits. Yoga provided another community; it had somewhat become a part of my identity, and it was a lifestyle. However, I trusted that by removing this competing branch, I wasn't being deprived of something, but saved from something. God always has a better plan. I know God's pruning is always for my good. Pruning is not punishment; it's love. God didn't want anything in my life that seemed beneficial on the outside to corrupt what He was doing on the inside.

If you practice yoga and feel triggered when people ask you about it, if you dabble in the New Age, or are engaged in ANYTHING that has caused personal conviction, then that's a part of the pruning process. Trust the pruning. Cutting off the competing branch can be hard, I know, especially when you feel like you are getting something out of it, but you can't always trust your feelings. If we always pursued everything that felt good, we'd be in a world of hurt. When God is trying to prune things out of your life, it is not the time to look inward to rationalize; it's the time to look upward. Don't let your own rationale talk you out of lifting your eyes to the hills where your help comes from (Psalm 121:1, paraphrased).

We aren't meant to be independent from God. We are not meant to be in control or do this life alone. God is in control. True freedom comes from letting God be on the throne where He belongs, and letting Him lead. I learned to let go of the belief that I had everything under control, which was difficult. Before my yoga pruning season I used to make excuses like: *"I'm only exercising; I'm not doing the other stuff. I have it all under control. My intentions are pure. God knows my heart."* Man, that competing branch was growing. I'm so glad I allowed God to prune it away. If you allow Him to prune what doesn't belong, know that you are allowing Him to make room for something healthy to grow in its place.

SELF-CARE

I t may seem unusual to shift from discussing the dangers of self-reliance to highlighting the importance of self-care, but self-care, when viewed through a Biblical lens, is not an act of self-sufficiency; on the contrary, it is a form of stewardship.

Many people view self-care as just taking care of their bodies or relaxing after a stressful day, and, while these elements can contribute to care, they do not encompass a "whole"listic meaning of self-care. Biblical self-care digs deeper; it goes beyond the superficial practices, because taking care of yourself involves more than just feeling good; it's about stewarding what God has given you, which is a mind, body, and spirit.

The world does a disservice by presenting self-care like a checklist of things to do to the body, making it the main character, but if you only focus on your body, you neglect two-thirds of who you are, and neglecting that much of yourself is crazy. We are not just flesh and bones; we are thinking, feeling, and spiritual beings, and each part requires attention.

Learning To Water The Whole You

I was born in Queens, New York, raised on Hollis Ave, and I can say without a doubt that we had the best yard on our block. My grandfather kept the grass in our front and backyard immaculate, and he also cared for a flourishing garden. My grandfather grew tomatoes along the fence, and in the very back section of our yard, he grew a variety of vegetables and leafy greens. I remember watching him tend to the garden as I played in the backyard. Sometimes, I would help, and sometimes, I was busy doing my own thing, but one thing I stopped everything for was running through the sprinklers on a hot summer day while the garden and grass were being watered. As I recall this memory of pure and simple happiness, I wonder, what if my grandfather focused solely on the tomatoes and only watered that section of the garden while neglecting all the beautiful, delicious greens? The tomatoes would have thrived, but the mustards, collards, and other plants would have been left to wither. In this same way we are called to tend to our whole garden if we want it to thrive. Our "garden" is our mind, body, and spirit. When you water, tend to, and care for yourself, you create an environment where every part of you can flourish like God designed.

Mind, Body, Spirit In The Word Of God

You don't have to go outside of Christianity to care for your mental, physical, and spiritual health. The Bible acknowledges them all under the umbrella of God's infallible Word.

The Bible highlights the importance of renewing and disciplining the mind. We are called to reject the patterns of this world and allow God to transform us from the inside out. "Don't copy the behavior and customs of this world, but let God transform you into a new person by changing the way you think. Then you will learn to know God's will for you, which is good and pleasing and perfect" (Romans 12:2 NLT). This process involves examining your thoughts, beliefs, and attitudes. David shows us how as he prays the perfect prayer of introspection, "Search me, O God, and know my heart; try me, and know my anxieties; and see if there is any wicked way in me, and lead me in the way everlasting" (Psalm 139:23-24 NKJV). Paul echoes a similar directive by urging us to take every thought captive and make it obedient to Christ (2 Corinthians 10:5, paraphrased). Why so much focus on the mind, will, and emotions? Because what we choose to focus on influences not just our emotional health and well-being but our spiritual health as well (there's that interconnectedness). This is why Paul tells us what to think about, "Finally, brethren, whatever things *are* true, whatever things *are* noble, whatever things *are* just, whatever things *are* pure, whatever things *are* lovely, whatever things *are* of good report, if *there* is any virtue and if *there* is anything praiseworthy— meditate on these things" (Philippians 4:8 NKJV).

Then there is the body. God cares as much about our bodies as He does about our minds. So much so that scripture tells us our bodies are sacred. "Do you not know that your body is the temple of the Holy Spirit *who is* in you, whom you have from God, and you are not your own? For you were bought at a price; therefore glorify God in your body and in your spirit, which are God's" (1 Corinthians 6:19-20 NKJV).

Paul informs us that our body is a temple of the Holy Spirit, and then goes on to emphasize the importance of glorifying God with both our body and spirit. Glorifying God involves honoring, praising, and worshiping Him. While we often associate honor, praise, and worship with verbal expressions, Paul instead says we are to honor, praise, and glorify God with our entire body. It's not just about the words we speak. God's Word is telling us that we must use literally our whole body and figuratively our whole being to glorify Him. And, not just our body but our Spirit too. Jesus Himself states that both the body and spirit must be acknowledged and tended to in Matthew 4:4. Jesus says, "Man shall not live by bread alone, but by every Word that comes from the mouth of God." Jesus makes it clear that life is not sustained by physical food alone, but by spiritual nourishment, highlighting the interconnectedness of body and spirit.

Mind, body, and spiritual health is whole person health. God doesn't only care about our spirit or our mind, He desires to connect with every part of our being. Paul prays this in 1 Thessalonians 5:23 (ESV) saying: "Now may the God of peace himself sanctify you completely, and may your whole spirit and soul and body be kept blameless at the coming of our Lord Jesus Christ."

Here are some questions you can ask yourself to help engage with your mind, body, and spirit. You might use these questions as prompts for journal entries, reflect on them during prayer, or carry one question from each section with you throughout your day as a reminder to be mindful.

Mind, Will & Emotions (Soul)

1. How can I renew my mind with truth today?

2. What lies am I tempted to believe today based on where my thoughts have been lingering, and how can I replace them with God's Word?

3. How can I align my desires with God's will today?

4. What emotions do I need to bring to God today instead of managing alone?

5. What Scriptures can I meditate on to anchor my mind and heart today?

6. How can I be mindful to align my choices to reflect a surrendered will to Christ?

7. How can I create mental space to hear God more clearly today?

8. How can I be honest with God about my thoughts and feelings today?

9. How can I become more aware of the thoughts, desires, and emotions that will shape my responses today?

10. How can I guard my mind today by filtering my thoughts through truth, not emotion or assumption?

11. How can I practice grace toward myself today?

Body

1. How can I steward my physical health in a way that honors God today?

2. What boundaries can I set to help my body rest and recover today?

3. How can I use my physical strength to serve others today?

4. What does it look like to glorify God in or with my body today?

5. Is there anything I need to release physically (stress, tension, fatigue)?

6. How can I align my actions with the truth that my body is God's temple?

7. What habits can I practice today that promote long-term health and energy?

8. What does rest look like for my body today?

9. How can I move my body today in gratitude rather than punishment?

Spirit

1. How can I remain connected to the Vine (Jesus) today?

2. What fruit of the Spirit do I want to cultivate today?

3. How can I posture my heart to listen to the Holy Spirit today?

4. What spiritual discipline is God inviting me to lean into

today (prayer, fasting, worship, etc.)?

5. How can I hunger and thirst for righteousness today?

6. What promise of God do I need to cling to today?

7. How can I respond to spiritual conviction with repentance and grace today?

8. In what way can I live out my identity as a new creation today?

9. How can I walk in alignment with the Spirit instead of striving in my own strength?

MIND, BODY, SPIRIT - GOD'S WAY

INTENTIONAL TIME WITH GOD

In a world filled with noise, distractions, and busyness, it's easy to overlook the one thing we need most as children of God: intentional time in His presence, more specifically, daily intentional time in His presence. This chapter is an invitation to slow down and to be still.

I wonder if, after hearing about the importance of spending intentional time with God, you might be thinking, *Well, that sounds great, but what does that mean for me in my everyday life? How am I supposed to fit this into my schedule? Why does it matter?* If one of those thoughts has crossed your mind, you're not alone. Those are fair questions, and I'm going to do my best to answer them. First, let's start by asking, what does God's Word specifically say about spending time with Him? This way, we aren't basing anything on personal opinions or experiences, but instead going straight to the source of truth.

Let's turn to Matthew 6:6 (NKJV) where Jesus says, "But you, when you pray, go into your room, and when you have shut your door, pray to your Father who *is* in the *secret place*; and your Father who sees in secret will reward you openly." Right here, we see a clear example of the value God places on private, intentional time with Him. Notice that Jesus doesn't say, "If you pray," but "When you pray." There's an assumption that this practice is not optional but essential.

Now, you might say, "Okay, Jesus says to pray, but does it have to be intentional or structured? Isn't praying on the go or thinking about God while I'm driving enough?" That's a great question. Yes, God is everywhere, and He hears us wherever we are. However, just like any relationship, quality time matters. Think about your closest relationship. If you only spoke to that person in passing or while multitasking, how deep would that relationship be? God desires a relationship with us that goes beyond surface-level interactions.

Let's talk about barriers because I know you might be thinking: *I'm busy. My days are packed, and there's hardly a moment to breathe, let alone carve out dedicated time for God.* Trust me, I get it. But, spending intentional time with God isn't about adding another task to your to-do list, or squeezing one more thing into your already jam-packed day, it's only about reprioritizing your day around what truly matters.

Have you ever heard the rock, pebbles, and sand story? It

is often used as an illustration to talk about priorities and time management. Imagine you're holding an empty jar, and the goal is to fit big rocks, pebbles, and sand into it. If you start with the sand and pebbles, there won't be room for the big rocks. But, if you start by placing the big rocks in the jar first, then the pebbles and sand can fill in around them. The big rocks are the important things in life, so spending intentional time with God is a "big rock." When you put Him first, everything else has a way of falling into place.

Start small. If you're not used to setting aside time with God, don't feel like you need to spend an hour or two a day praying and reading your Bible. Begin with ten to fifteen minutes. Find a quiet place and open your Bible.

The beauty of spending intentional time with God is that it's not about perfection; it's about being in His presence. God isn't keeping score or waiting for you to check off a box. He's waiting to meet with you, to speak to your heart, and to pour His love into your life. When you give Him your undivided attention, even if only for a few minutes to start, you'll find that He meets you exactly where you are.

Spending intentional time with God transforms everything. When you make time to connect with Him, you are reminded of who you are and whose you are. You are reminded of the truth, your authority through Christ, hope, promise, whatever you need to be better equipped.

Remember in John 15:5 (NIV), Jesus says, "I am the vine; you are the branches. If you remain in me and I in you, you will bear much fruit; apart from me you can do nothing." Intentional time with God is how we remain in Him. It's how we stay connected to the Source of life, strength, and purpose.

Don't settle for just getting through the day. Make time to be still, to listen, to pray, and to rest in God's presence. Not out of obligation, but out of a desire to know Him more deeply and to let His love consume you. Psalms 46:10 (ESV), "Be still, and know that I am God." The phrase "be still" invites us to cease, to intentionally stop trying to be strong and handling it all on our own, to weaken ourselves, and become helpless. Why? Because it's in those moments of stillness, of ceasing our agenda, that we know that He is God. Lean into His presence, His peace, His guidance, His voice. Start today, right where you are. God is waiting to meet you.

If you're going to start a new habit, the best time to start is in the morning. Wake up 15–30 minutes earlier to read, journal, pray, and most importantly, sit in silence and listen. This intentional start to your day prioritizes God, which sets your mindset for the day. Intentional daily time with God each morning changed my whole Christian walk. I genuinely questioned how I had lived so much of my life without doing this. It was a game-changer.

You could also use this time to journal your prayers. It could be a letter, honestly expressing your fears or doubts, showing gratitude, or asking questions. Again, the most important thing is making sure you end with quiet time to listen.

Throughout your day, make space for worship and reflection. Play a worship song during your commute or chores. You can also take a walk with God. Literally, go for a walk and talk to Him. Or, in the evening, take time to review your day.

These suggestions are not all or nothing; you should pick what works for you. Start somewhere, even if it's small at first, because starting with just five minutes a day is better than sitting down for one hour once a week.

MEDITATION

Should Christians meditate? Let me make this incredibly simple, because sometimes questions like this are answered in a roundabout way. I'm here to shout a definitive YES from the mountaintops.

You may have shied away from meditation for fear it's too closely related to New Age philosophies. Or you may feel it just isn't a Biblical approach. Or maybe you know that God calls us to meditate, but you don't think you know how. Maybe you've tried before, and it just didn't work for you.

Well, I want to talk about meditation and provide five Scriptures that highlight its role in the Bible. Meditation is not only beneficial but essential for Christians. God repeatedly talks

111

about meditation in His Word:

1. **Joshua 1:8 (NKJV):** "This Book of the Law shall not depart from your mouth, but you[a] shall meditate in it day and night, that you may observe to do according to all that is written in it. For then you will make your way prosperous, and then you will have good success."

2. **Psalm 1:2-3 (NLT):** "But they delight in the law of the Lord, meditating on it day and night. They are like trees planted along the riverbank, bearing fruit each season. Their leaves never wither, and they prosper in all they do."

3. **Psalm 19:14 (NKJV):** "Let the words of my mouth and the meditation of my heart be acceptable in Your sight, O Lord, my [a]strength and my Redeemer."

4. **Psalm 119:15 (NLT):** I will study your commandments and reflect on your ways.

5. **Philippians 4:8 (NKJV):** "Finally, brethren, whatever things *are* true, whatever things *are* noble, whatever things *are* just, whatever things *are* pure, whatever things *are* lovely, whatever things *are* of good report, if *there is* any virtue and if *there is* anything praiseworthy—meditate on these things."

As a Bible-believing Christian, meditation is a tool for your use. I like to think of it as a spiritual weapon in your arsenal. When you pull it out and use it correctly, meditation will set you up to put the Word of God into practice. This will help you purify your life, separate you from the world's way of thinking,

 MIND, BODY, SPIRIT - GOD'S WAY

give glory to God, deepen your understanding of the Bible, cultivate virtues that align with the fruits of the Spirit, lead you into your purpose, and inevitably, draw you closer to God in all areas of your life through His Son, Jesus.

We aim to align our minds and our hearts with the God of the Bible, not the universe or any type of energy. While it may seem harmless to use certain spiritual terms in a trendy or casual way, doing so can slowly reshape how you understand God and His nature. Language shapes perspective, and when those shifts go unnoticed, they can open the door to subtle misunderstandings. This is something to be mindful of, especially in a culture where truth is easily blurred. This is why for some, meditation has a negative connotation. Many people lean more toward the idea that meditation is done with an Eastern mindset. Eastern meditation seeks to transcend the self through one's "own" strength and attain union with the divine by emptying the mind.

Meditating on the Word of God and learning to align your thoughts with God's thoughts, however, is something completely different. In Biblical meditation, God gives us a point of a reference. The goal here is to take His Word, reflect on it, and internalize it with the ultimate purpose of applying it. This is what meditating should look like. You are not looking to empty your mind; you are looking to fill it. Let your mind do what God created it to do. He did not design our brains to be void of thought. Why do you think it's so hard to clear your mind? It's because your brain was designed to think. Then, what do most people do? They take what the world says about meditation, and when they struggle to empty their mind, they either give up or find a different way to achieve their goal by engaging in yoga or some other facet of meditation, which takes them down a path God never intended for them to go.

What would it look like if you didn't beat yourself up for not being able to clear your mind? Instead, you thanked God that your brain is operating the way He intended for it to operate, and you gave Him thanks that your brain is actually working. What would it look like if you learned to meditate the way the Bible tells us to? What would it look like if you embraced God's way of meditation?

Let's go back to the book of Joshua. Moses had just died, and Joshua was appointed the new leader of Israel. Those were some huge shoes to fill. I'm not sure about you, but stepping in behind someone who God spoke to from a burning bush, who God used to lead his people out from the tyranny of Pharaoh, who had a staff turn into a serpent, who parted the Red Sea, who received the Ten Commandments from God, and whose face shone with the glory of God, just to name a few things, is pretty intimidating. This may be why God, in His love, His mercy, and His grace, encouraged Joshua so heavily.

In Joshua chapter 1, God affirms Joshua by speaking life into him, prophesying over him, making a promise to him, and then, after all that, commanding him to go. In the midst of all this, we find verse 8 (NIV): "Keep this Book of the Law always on your lips; meditate on it day and night, so that you may be careful to do everything written in it. Then you will be prosperous and successful." God gave Joshua directives and then told him to meditate on the Word? Why? The promise attached to it was that God would then make Joshua's way prosperous and that he would be successful. Meditating on Scripture by mulling it over and allowing it to permeate your thoughts and feelings renews your mind, shapes your thoughts, and changes your actions. This is the foundation of Christian living.

I have heard it explained like this. Meditation is like tuning a radio to a specific station. You are bypassing all the other frequencies with one station in mind, God's station. When you tune into God's station, you seek to clearly hear His voice. This is what aligns your heart with His message. Just like a radio needs to be on the right frequency to pick up a clear signal to reach the intended destination, so do we. In contrast, Eastern meditation is like turning off the radio entirely and hoping that in the silence, you discover something deeper within yourself. For us as Christians, the focus is not on silence and definitely not on self, but on what God says in His Word.

Now, there is nothing wrong with tuning out distractions with the intended purpose of being able to focus, but the brain is going to think, so you should tell it what to think about rather than just accepting whatever thought lands in your mind. Learn to think, slowly and carefully, about what the Word of God says.

There are two main definitions in the Bible for the word meditation. One is found in Psalm 5:1-3; the word meditate here means groaning, similar to a low utterance. The other is one I listed in the beginning of this chapter, and it can be found in Psalm 1:2-3. The word meditate here means to ruminate (like a cow does).

Thinking slowly and carefully about the Word of God has been compared to the cow's process of digesting food. If you are wondering what that means, you aren't alone. I'm from the city, so farm analogies were not a part of my day to day. I had to look up how cows eat. Let me break it down for you, and if you're a farmer, bear with me. I think it's a really interesting process and quite detailed. God didn't have to make cows go through all this to eat, so I wonder if He created them this way as a picture for us. I don't know, but here's the process:

Cows were made to eat grass and hay, which is really fibrous; therefore, they were designed with a specialized digestive system that requires some extra steps to extract the most nutrients from their diet. Because they can't digest their food all at once, they need a little help breaking it down. This is where it gets gross, but stick with me, I'm proving a point.

After a cow eats, their food travels to a special part of their stomach, and when they feel ready, they regurgitate the partially digested food back into their mouth to chew some more. I know. I know.

The process of the cow rechewing the hay/grass is called "chewing the cud." As the cow chews its food again, it breaks the food down into smaller pieces, which helps digest it. This repeated chewing process not only allows the cow to extract even more nutrients from the food, but I also learned that it helps the cow remain calm and relaxed.

The practice of meditation is designed to not only strengthen your relationship with God by drawing you closer to His Word, but it provides greater clarity, which gives you peace that surpasses all understanding, just like in Philippians 4:7 (paraphrased), and this will help you process life's challenges by focusing on what God says. When you "chew" on God's Word and allow it to nourish you, it deepens your understanding, and with that, it brings a sense of calm and clarity, because when you meditate on Him, you train your mind to think about things through the lens of truth and not self. Your heart is self, and as stated in Jeremiah, the heart is hopelessly dark and deceitful, a puzzle that no one can figure out. So, why follow the trends of the world? Why would you go and seek out your own self for answers or peace?

This is why God directed Joshua to meditate on His Word. It wasn't enough for him to just be encouraged through prophecy and promises, he had to continue to get the Word, the laws, and the precepts of God deep within him to prosper in the way God intended for him to prosper. Just as a cow extracts the maximum amount of nutrients from its food by bringing it back up again, meditating on God's Word in this same way allows God's truth to fully nourish your mind, body, and spirit.

Journey Into Meditation

Think of this as a starting point, as an a la carte list of options. You can choose one or all. This is not so much a "how to meditate in order" but more of a flexible framework for which to create your own meditative practice within a Biblical framework.

God created us all differently, so what works for some may not work for all. Be uniquely you and find what works (as long as it stays within the context of Scripture).

1. Prepare Your Heart

Decide to meditate. Choose a Scripture to think about throughout the day. Silently recite it to yourself and think about how you can apply it to your day.

2. Shift Your Mindset

Remind yourself that this time is about drawing closer to God and aligning with His truth, not about silence or self-reflection.

3. Prepare An Environment

Find yourself a quiet space. Choose a space free from distractions or one that has limited distractions. Sometimes, you have to create a space in the midst of distraction. For example, one of my go to tactics is using headphones to play music in the background.

4. Journal

This can help clear your mind from all the things, the cares, and the worries of the day. This is not the same as clearing your mind. Think of this as more of handing over the things that are at the forefront of your mind so you can create space to hear from God.

    MIND, BODY, SPIRIT - GOD'S WAY

5. Have Your Bible Close By

Ask the Holy Spirit to lead you to a verse, passage, or chapter. Remember: one verse is okay. It's manageable, and a single verse can make room for deeper reflection.

6. Read Slowly and Carefully

Wherever you feel led to go, read the passage aloud or silently a few times. Do any words or phrases really stand out to you? Or, do you feel called to seek to gain a fuller understanding of what you read?

7. Reflect and "Chew" on the Word

"Chew the cud." Break down what you read into smaller parts. Choose a verse or two and think about what its saying. Think about the meaning and significance. Ask questions: What is this teaching me about God and His nature? Ponder on that.

8. Memorization

Select a verse that resonates with you and memorize it. Write it down on an index card or on your phone and go back to it throughout the day, repeating the verse and testing yourself. I've also seen people write the first letter of each word down as a mnemonic device.

9. Pray the Word

Turn the verse you chose or felt led to into a prayer. For example, if you're meditating on Psalm 94:19, you might pray: "Lord, I feel my anxious thoughts increasing, but Your Word reminds me that it's the comfort of Your presence that calms me down. Thank You for a way out. Help me not to be anxious but to bring my requests and worries to You with thanksgiving. Thank You for the promise to bring delight to my soul."

10. Apply the Truth

Contemplate on how your time in the Word challenges or encourages you to live differently. Write down one specific action step you can take. Just a baby step based on what you've meditated on.

11. Follow-up

Throughout the day or week, return to the verse or passage you've been meditating on to reflect further. Ask the Holy Spirit to speak to you, and allow new insights to develop as you continue to "chew" on the Word.

However, you choose to meditate when you are done. Rest. Thank God for His Word, for speaking to you through His Word, and for His presence. Rest in the peace that comes from focusing on His truth. Just be. It is His Word that's alive and active, so it will accomplish what He set out for it to accomplish (Hebrews 4:12 NIV, paraphrased). You've done your part, which is hiding the Word of God in your heart (Psalm 119:11, paraphrased).

BREATHWORK VS. DEEP BREATHING EXERCISES (STRESS REDUCTION)

hat about the breathwork aspect of yoga?

Breathing is just breathing, right? And, even if yoga and the Bible contradict each other, isn't learning how to breathe beneficial to overall wellness? The answer is yes! Breathing is a necessary component of life; it's crucial. Breathing is LIFE, and it's hard to focus on wellness when you're not, you know, alive. However, when it comes to breathwork in yoga and learning how to breathe for stress reduction, those are two very different things. Breathing to calm the nervous system relaxes the body and reduces stress responses. Breathwork, on the other hand, is the fourth limb of yoga, following asanas (the physical postures), and it serves a specific purpose. One is biological and one is spiritual.

Let's start with the goal of breathwork in yoga. Your breath in yoga is called Pranayama. It is a Sanskrit word that refers to the practice of breath control in yoga. "Prana" means life force, and "yama" means control or discipline. Although breath control or Pranayama offers both physical and mental benefits, in yoga, its deeper purpose is spiritual. Breathing in yoga serves as a vital tool; it serves as the path to self-realization and the union with the divine or higher self.

I want to share a passage from B.K.S. Iyenger's *Light on Yoga*, in which Pranayama (breath control) is discussed: "Every living creature unconsciously breathes the prayer 'So'ham' (Sah = He: Aham = I – He, the Immortal Spirit, am I) with each inward breath. So also with each outgoing breath, each creature prays 'Hamsah' (I am He).[1]" The belief expressed in "*So'ham*" is, I am He; I am the Divine, so when you are engaging in breathwork, this is the belief behind the breath.

Breathwork also depends on what type of yoga you're engaged in at the moment. For example, are you practicing Hatha or Kundalini? I previously discussed Kundalini, explaining that this kind of yoga believes that dormant serpent energy is coiled at the base of the spine. When someone guides you through Kundalini breathwork, the goal is to channel that energy up the spine and throughout the body. I continue to emphasize this style of yoga because it serves as an open door, inviting the spirit of Kundalini to enter. In Hatha yoga, breathwork is used to experience a spiritual awakening and enhanced self-realization. Through disciplined Pranayama, or breathwork practice, the goal is to access deeper states of consciousness, expand awareness, and experience profound states of inner peace and unity with the divine. Breathwork is seen as part of the breath of the universal spirit. And you thought it was "just breathing" in a yoga class. Well, to be fair, if you have ever taken a yoga class, you may have been just breathing, but the intention of the practice remains the same, whether you are aware of it or not.

I came across an old video featuring Madonna and highlighting her newly found yoga practice. She brought attention to the practice of yoga in the West during several prime-time television interviews. One interview was with Oprah, and she kept referring to yoga as a workout, insinuating it was just a different type of exercise. In another interview with Rosie O'Donnell, she talked Rosie into "doing yoga." Madonna then placed a black crown of thorns on Rosie's head and prompted her into Ujjayi breathing. Now let's just pause there for a little while. Why would a "workout" require this? I'll continue. Rosie's response to hearing this type of breathing for the first time was comical to the audience, yet insightful to me. Rosie's response to the Ujjayi breathing was, "It sounds like Satan making a cappuccino." Out of all the metaphors she could have chosen, that one revealed something deeper. Bypassing her statement, Madonna then began to walk her through a sun salutation.[2]

I share this to try and paint a picture that no matter what kind of breathwork you are engaged in, it goes beyond mere relaxation if it's through yoga or any other New Age practice.

In yoga, the focus is on the idea that your breath leads you into a heightened awareness. It's spiritual, not physical. It's a conduit. The goal here is not to be afraid of breathing or to be apprehensive about using your breath while exercising or to relax the nervous system. I want to help you understand the difference between when someone is trying to lead you into an altered state and when you are, in fact, just breathing.

Some examples of breathwork may be: to visualize energy in your body, you may be prompted to inhale through your sacrum, you may be encouraged to imagine things and then let go of all the images, or you may hear things like, *empty your mind of thoughts and words*, or *let your mind be filled with breath and silence*. Different people will express things in their own unique ways, so while I'm not aware of a standard script for breathwork in yoga, when you are being led in it, you can sense the difference.

Deep breathing for relaxation and/or stress reduction will sound more like guiding you through natural breathing. You may be instructed to breathe through your nose and exhale through your mouth, fill your lungs with air and exhale, or you may be guided through a progressive muscle relaxation. Depending on the instructor, you may even hear these same prompts in a yoga class, but the difference is the intent. Breathwork is about controlling energy in the body and clearing pathways (chakra stuff), and ultimately helping with deep focus and meditation. The goal of deep breathing exercises is to relax the body, to get you out of your sympathetic nervous system (the state of high alert), and into your parasympathetic nervous system (a state of relaxation).

Now, to be fair, yoga addresses the nervous system as well, but it's not without all the other things attached to it. Deep breathing calms the nervous system without any attachments. It's not only beneficial for your physical and mental health but also calms stress and anxiety and can lower your blood pressure. The goal here is to train yourself to open your lungs to breathe more efficiently.

Some might believe that breathwork and deep breathing are just different terms for the same concept, but its not just semantics. Breathwork in yoga is not used for relaxation. Relaxation may be the immediate byproduct of engaging in breathwork, but as a Christian, you have to ask yourself, are the long-term effects worth the short-term benefits? Breathwork in yoga goes beyond simply experiencing the benefits of deep breathing; it is opening yourself spiritually.

TESTIMONIALS

Here are the stories of four Christian women who were once deeply involved in the world of yoga. Each one entered that space searching for peace, healing, or clarity, never imagining they were stepping into spiritual territory far from the truth. But God, in His mercy, met them right where they were. What follows are testimonies of how He gently and powerfully brought them out of deception and into a place of truth, repentance, and recommitment to Jesus Christ.

Debbie's Story

"I didn't realize how far I had gone," she said. "But God is so faithful. He brought the right people into my life at just the right time. And He loved me enough to pull me out. I thought that I could really compartmentalize it… that I could go on the retreats and just separate it. But you can't."

As Debbie reflected on how she found herself in the midst of a lifestyle that didn't align with her deeply held beliefs, she went on to say, "I never went looking for yoga." Debbie shared that her yoga journey started in a totally unexpected way when she needed a new place to live. "In 2022, I was looking for a new roommate. I ended up finding a girl through a local Facebook group. We met up, connected, and she invited me to move in."

Debbie shared that her new roommate was deep into yoga. "She invited me to do yoga with her, and I didn't think anything of it. Honestly, it felt good, peaceful. And when she told me about a yoga retreat happening in Georgia, I thought, 'Why not?' She needed an assistant, so I got to go for free."

That retreat marked the beginning of a new chapter for Debbie. "I was going through a lot during that time," she said. "And I felt like I had found healing. People were kind. It felt safe. Peaceful. I thought, 'This is good.'"

But what Debbie didn't realize was that the more she said yes to the retreats, the deeper she was being pulled into something she didn't fully understand. Debbie began traveling to retreats around the world, the Galapagos Islands, Colorado, and eventually Greece. Each one introduced new practices, new philosophies, and, slowly, new belief systems.

"In the Galapagos, I was introduced to Chi Gong," she said. "It's like breathwork mixed with energy movement. They say it cleanses the body energetically. It felt peaceful. I didn't know it was spiritual."

Debbie shared that at every retreat, yoga was just the surface. "Before sessions, the instructor would sage everyone, use animal spirit cards, and offer words for the day. She'd go person by person and wave sage around their bodies. I didn't know what that was about. I just thought it was part of the practice. We'd also pick cards, animal spirit cards, and she'd read the meanings. Again, I didn't think anything was wrong with it."

But as time went on, Debbie began to notice how accepting she was becoming to things that, years earlier, would have felt off-limits. "I started carrying crystals, rose quartz to attract love, and green ones for abundance. I had no idea that this was sin. I would even 'charge' my crystals in the moonlight and charge water with moon energy. I thought it was symbolic. I didn't realize I was participating in witchcraft."

Debbie also began wearing malas (Hindu prayer beads), practiced tapping techniques, and took Ayurvedic cooking classes that taught spiritual eating based on body types and energies. She did energy-cleansing and Reiki sessions to remove fear and emotional blocks. At one retreat, she even participated in a practice called Hapé, a tobacco-based snuff used for spiritual ceremonies.

"It was like a slow fade," she said. "One thing led to another. And the whole time, I thought I was just taking care of myself."

What's important to mention is that even though Debbie was immersed in the yoga community, she still considered herself a Christian. She had grown up Methodist, was baptized in 2006 at a non-denominational church, and in 2021 she started attending the church she considers home in Florida.

"I never left my faith. I was still praying. I was still attending church. But I thought I could separate the two."

But, the deeper Debbie grew in her walk with Jesus, the more conflicted she became. "There was a moment in Greece," she said, "I remember waking up and the first thing I saw every morning was this big, beautiful church right outside the retreat center. I felt like God was showing me something. I just didn't want to listen yet."

Then she met me. She said I gently confronted her about the path she was taking. "You told me, 'Don't go on the next retreat,'"

Debbie continued, "But I had already paid." she said. In her mind, she decided, "I'll just compartmentalize it. I'll do the retreat but keep it separate." I thought that was possible, but I was wrong.

Debbie shared that at her Bible study, she explained that more women started asking questions. Some even shared their own testimonies of how God had told them to walk away. Even in that moment, Debbie reported her response was "I felt maybe God had called me to the yoga community so that I could help teach them about God. And our yoga teacher always talks about Jesus." On the other hand, Debbie recalled that she also talked about Mother Earth, Mother Gaia, and all of these other things.

Debbie went on, "So the deeper that I get into my Christianity, and reading my Bible, and talking with other Christians about it, the more I'm realizing that you can't separate the two."

Debbie's journey continues as she mentioned, "One night, someone recommended a book: *He Came to Set the Captives Free.* I didn't even order it on purpose. I was just looking at it on Amazon, and the next thing I knew, I got a confirmation that it had shipped. The book showed up at my door the next day."

Debbie stated that she read the entire book in two hours, and it brought clarity. "It opened my eyes. I was doing things that were deeply spiritual and not in a good way. Even though it looked like healing, it was deception. And once I saw it, I couldn't unsee it."

That was the moment Debbie started cleaning out everything. "I got rid of the malas. I gathered up the crystals. I threw away the cards. I stopped attending the retreats. I knew it had to be a clean break. I couldn't keep straddling the fence. But it wasn't easy. That was my whole community," she said. "Those were all my friends. It was my social circle, my business network, and my comfort zone. Walking away felt like losing everything. But I knew I had to choose God."

Her message to others is simple:

"You've got to really search your heart. Is what you're getting out of this worth risking eternity? Because I'm telling you it opens doors. Whether you believe that or not doesn't change the fact that it does."

She continued, "The enemy doesn't come in wearing horns. He comes in through things that look like light, like healing, wellness, or self-love. But those things lead to bondage if they're outside of Christ."

Kristel's Story

"The devil had been toying with me since I was a kid," Kristel reflects. "And I didn't even know it."

Kristel's words echoed as she shared that she didn't start her life deeply immersed in Christianity as she knows it today, rooted in relationship, grace, mercy, and love. She described her Catholic family as "CEO's" Christmas and Easter Only. She said their faith was "more of a twice-a-year tradition than a way of life." After her parents divorced when she was just six years old, even those twice-a-year visits stopped. Kristel recalls just a year of catechism as a child, which she described as "barely enough to lay a foundation." So, for most of her life, Kristel described herself as "spiritually vulnerable."

She self-identified as double-minded in her relationship with God. "I'd talk to God, I'd pray, but I was still living in the world. I wasn't lukewarm, I didn't even know better. I didn't know the truth."

Kristel's introduction to yoga came through her sister, sharing that they both struggled with depression, and her sister, who discovered yoga in college, encouraged her to give it a try. So when Kristel saw that her college offered yoga as an elective class, she signed up.

"I came from a dance background, so yoga just felt natural," she recalls. "It was stretching, moving, and breathing; it made me feel good. And at the time, I truly believed it was helping me stay out of that depressive place."

At first, it was just about physical fitness. However, yoga gradually became a spiritual gateway. Kristel shared that she was introduced to crystals, sage, palo santo, and sound bowls. She began fusing wellness with spiritual ideas, some from yoga philosophy and others from New Age teachings. "I was completely deceived. I thought all of it was light, healing, and good. But I now know how wrong I was."

Over time, Kristel started practicing Reiki and eventually became certified, starting with level one in 2018, and continuing up through multiple levels.

"There was this whole little incantation at the beginning of Reiki sessions," she explains. "You'd open yourself up to become a channel for healing energy, but you weren't calling on Jesus. You were calling on some vague 'higher power.' And that right there was the problem."

She describes feeling sensations that seemed good and light at the time, but in hindsight, she believes they were counterfeit. "The enemy mimics the Holy Spirit. So even though it felt peaceful, it wasn't holy peace. It was a counterfeit peace. I was giving myself away, letting myself be used without realizing who I was giving access to."

Kristel remembers going on to use sound bowls and also trying Kundalini yoga once with her Reiki instructor and then again alone.

"That second time, I felt darkness. I could feel it. The veil was thin. I knew immediately: this is not for me."

She also tried tarot cards, shadow work, and even consulted mediums. Looking back, she sees how all of it was interconnected and dangerous. "It was all counterfeit. The enemy is so uncreative—he takes what God gave us and just distorts it. He twists it into something to serve him instead of God."

She went to share, while some of it started off casually or even jokingly, these practices gradually became normalized in her life. She once jokingly referred to herself as a "white witch"—believing she was doing good things, not realizing it was all a distortion of truth.

"I used to love anything witchy. Sabrina the Teenage Witch, spells, and energy work. I thought, 'It's all positive.' But I didn't know that I had opened door after door for the enemy to enter my life."

She later realized these influences weren't just random interests, they were generational. Coming from a Filipino background where she reports spiritualism and superstition are culturally embedded, Kristel had unknowingly inherited some of the spiritual practices passed down through her family.

In 2021, after years of practicing yoga off and on, Kristel finally completed her Yoga Teacher Training (YTT). Though she identified as a Christian, she had never read the Bible. "No one in my life ever told me not to do it. Not my family. Not the churches I went to. I didn't know the Word, so I didn't have discernment."

She recalls an assignment in college where she read an article warning Christians about yoga. "I disagreed with it. I actually wrote that yoga brought me closer to God. But looking back, I wasn't praying to Jesus in those classes. I was connecting with something, sure—but it wasn't Him."

Though she had all the training, Kristel shared that she never felt comfortable teaching yoga. "I'm a writer, not a speaker. I didn't want to cue movements or lead a class. So I shifted to sound healing. I thought, 'I really like sound bowls, I'll do that instead. So I shifted into sound healing instead. I invested hundreds of dollars into crystal sound bowls. I got certified. And it just kept going."

Each new practice felt like another rung on the ladder. Reiki, sound healing, energy work. "You feel like you have to keep going higher. But the ladder never ends."

In early 2023, Kristel's inner peace began to crack. She felt a deep spiritual heaviness, like she had felt during her most depressed years. One night, she lifted her hands while listening to *I Lift My Hands* by Chris Tomlin and cried out to God.

She believes that moment marked the beginning of her deliverance. Sharing that two weeks later, she reconnected with an old friend, a Christian who had also left the New Age. She continued on to describe their interaction. "Before I left her house, she felt this nudge from God to share everything with me. And she was battling with Him, like, 'I don't want to be the one to tell her.' But she obeyed. And I absorbed everything. She didn't have all the answers. But her obedience was enough to plant the seed."

Kristel immediately stopped everything: yoga, Reiki, sound bowls, crystals, and sage. She boxed it all up, even though she didn't yet understand why. "I didn't need to have the full explanation. I just knew I needed to stop. I boxed up my crystals. I stopped yoga. I didn't get rid of it all right away; it took time, but I stopped practicing. I told God, 'Until I know what's okay and what's not, I'm laying it all down.'"

She added, "Reiki was the hardest thing to let go of emotionally. I thought I was doing good, light things. But the light I felt wasn't from God. The funny thing is, I had peace during those 13 years. I credited yoga for not being depressed. But I know now it was all false. Because the moment I turned away from it, hell literally came for me."

What followed was six months of intense spiritual warfare. Kristel experienced fear, heaviness, confusion, and even physical oppression. "It felt like demons were just sitting on my chest when I woke up. My house was filled with darkness, and I didn't know how to get rid of it."

She realized that every object she had that was associated with the New Age and every practice she had embraced had opened a spiritual door. "Thank God, it's all in the dumpster now."

"The reason I knew it wasn't of God was because of what happened after I walked away. The torment. The backlash. Hell was mad I left, and that confirmed everything."

Kristel went on, "The confusion didn't lift overnight." She had to learn to hear God's voice, to read Scripture, to build the spiritual foundation she never had. "It was hard. But I knew God was leading me through it for a reason."

Now, with clearer eyes and a surrendered heart, she sees how deep the deception ran. Today, Kristel is walking in freedom. She's still healing, still learning, but she now has the discernment she didn't have for over a decade. And her story is a warning, and a part of her testimony.

"God allowed me to walk through deception so I could one day help deliver others out of it. That's why I share. That's why I thank God because He picked me up, turned me around, and opened my eyes."

Her message to others is simple:

"Take it to God. Ask Him. Lay it at His feet. If you don't know Jesus, start there. He wants a relationship with you. If you do know Him, then trust that He will reveal what you need to lay down."

"Yoga was the gateway drug for me. It opened every other spiritual door. I thought it was light. I thought it was peace. But it was false. The real peace didn't come until I surrendered it all to Jesus." She emphasizes that you may not get all the answers up front. But obedience is where the healing starts. "I didn't need a big why. The fact that the devil came after me so hard once I laid it down, that was all the confirmation I needed." And she added as a final word of caution, "If you're thinking of starting yoga, do something else."

Aleida's Story

"I was just doing it for the exercise. I wasn't doing it for spiritual reasons, and it still opened the door."

That's what Aleida told me when she shared her story of how yoga, something she once saw as harmless, gave the enemy access to her life. Before she ever called Jesus Lord, before she understood the spiritual realm, before she renounced anything, she thought she was just stretching.

At the start of Aleida's yoga journey, she was living in New York, going to undergrad, and working out regularly at the gym. Yoga was just part of the schedule.

"I literally was just doing it for physical fitness," she said. "They offered yoga classes through the gym, and I started going faithfully every week. Sometimes, even a couple times a week after work."

Aleida recalls the studio's appearance as unremarkable, sharing that "It wasn't decorated with statues or spiritual items. It was a clean gym environment, nothing outwardly spiritual, but there were moments, like at the end of class, when the instructor would read from a meditation or inspirational book." Aleida remembers being curious about it, but never followed up. She went on to describe her experience, stating, "She would read quotes after class while we were resting. That was the only thing I remember that was kind of extra outside of the exercise itself."

What Aleida didn't realize at the time was that her history had already laid a spiritual foundation that made her vulnerable to deception. Her upbringing was marked by a religious mixture and spiritual confusion.

"I grew up around psychics, tarot cards, and witchcraft books. I remember my brother's ex took me and my niece to a bookstore and bought us children's witchcraft books. I consumed that stuff. I read the spells, I said them out loud, but I didn't realize it was real." She also remembers consuming witchcraft-related media. "I used to love the movie *The Craft*. Even as a kid, I didn't think it was real. But I dabbled."

Aleida reported her family identified as Christian, but not in a surrendered or scripturally grounded way. "We went to church for holidays or special occasions. The church was dry. I didn't encounter God for myself."

After graduation, Aleida moved to Chicago for graduate school in her early twenties, and that's where she remembers everything changed for her. She went on stating, "One of my roommates was a Christian, and she invited me to church. That's how I got saved."

Even after coming to faith, she didn't immediately renounce her past involvement with yoga or the occult. Years passed before she began to learn about spiritual warfare, inner healing, and deliverance. "I started experiencing a lot of demonic things I hadn't experienced before I got saved: I started being attacked in my sleep, and having, like, sleep paralysis, and seeing spirits in my room. One night, I prayed against generational curses, and something came into my room, and my bed shook. I don't know if this is necessarily connected to yoga, but this is just kind of part of my story."

During that season, Aleida described seeking healing, deliverance, and breaking generational curses from her life. As she learned about opening spiritual doors and went through a list of things to renounce, she was surprised to find that yoga was on the list.

"It was just a long list, everything from horoscopes to witchcraft to yoga. I was renouncing everything, just going down the list."

Aleida went on to share that nothing happened until she got to Hinduism and Buddhism.

"That's when something started manifesting in me. I couldn't speak. I couldn't get the words out. Something was holding my tongue back. I was crying, trying to talk, but I physically couldn't. It was terrifying."

Aleida described this moment as terrifying, because she reported she did not feel "in control" of her body. She shared that eventually, the person she was praying with took spiritual authority over the situation, and she was able to break free and finish renouncing the practices. But the impact stuck with her.

"That was the moment I knew yoga opened a door. I never practiced Hinduism or Buddhism, but I did practice yoga. And something just didn't want to let go."

Aleida now speaks openly about the dangers of dismissing yoga as "just exercise," especially for Christian women.

"So many say, 'Oh, I just do it for the exercise,'" she said. "But I wasn't trying to connect to anything spiritual either, and it still opened a door. It gave the enemy access to my life."

Her message to others is simple:

"Seek answers. Seek the Lord. Ask Him about this. Because yoga doesn't align with the heart of God. Not because of how it's practiced, but because of what it's rooted in."

Nina's Story

"There was no chakra I could heal, no crystal I could grab, no affirmation I could say. The only thing I had was the name of Jesus."

Those were the words Nina spoke as she reflected on the moment when everything shifted for her, standing in a hospital hallway after being pushed out of the NICU as her son flatlined, feeling helpless as a Christian, a wife, and a new mother, realizing that the last year she had spent immersed in yoga, manifestation, and New Age healing practices meant nothing in that moment.

It was in the midst of this that Nina asked herself, "What have I been doing?" She described it as a moment when the light of God pierced through all the deception she had been living under.

"It's like being in darkness and the light is shown, and you're like, what? Like when the prodigal son was like, wait, why am I doing this? And he returned to his father."

Right then, the spiritual fog began to lift for Nina. She realized that everything she had been relying on—chakras, crystals, and affirmations—had no power to save her son or bring true peace. That moment in the NICU, watching doctors fight for her newborn son's life, shattered the illusion of control she thought she had, and there was a sharp transition from that point forward.

"I'm a very all-or-nothing person. I was like, get rid of it all. Renounce it all. Do away with it all." She didn't just stop practicing yoga and manifestation; she actively walked away and publicly renounced it all.

That was her breaking point, after she had been slowly, subtly, and gradually led off course; however, her story had begun years ago.

Nina's journey with yoga began during the pandemic, just as the world shut down. At the time, she was working as an online fitness coach.

"It started very progressively. I had started as a fitness coach, and when you explore online business, you get pushed into the mindset space, the self-development, and the self-improvement space. It's just riddled with a lot of New Age things." I think it's important to note that Nina considered herself a Christian her entire life. Her faith wasn't something she had abandoned; she just redefined her faith as she tried to cope with stress, anxiety, and depression.

Nina explained, "I was doing it under the guise of, 'I'm a Christian, I believe in Jesus. I've been a believer my whole life. But I never found practical ways to actually heal or deal with the stress, anxiety, and depression I was feeling. So even as a believer, I gravitated toward the New Age because it gave me tangible tools.'"

Nina didn't realize she was slowly blending truth with deception, and what began as fitness turned into something much more involved. "It's like what they call marijuana, a gateway drug. That's what yoga was for me."

She explained that once she got deeper into the online yoga community, it wasn't long before she was introduced to other spiritual practices. She went on to clarify. "Now I wasn't just stretching, I was healing chakras. Then I needed this stone, that stone. I got into crystals and orgonite. Then it turned into full-blown manifestation. I had a YouTube channel. I was teaching manifestation. I got a life coach certification, and the course was rooted in the New Age."

I asked Nina if anyone had ever cautioned her. Any Christian friends? Her husband? She shared, "My dad actually read an article once about yoga being a religion. I remember my sister and I saying, 'Okay, Dad, relax.' I wasn't even practicing yoga at the time, but when you're a teenager, you just brush it off." She then went on to share that at the height of her involvement, her husband had joined her in the practices, and the pandemic kept them isolated from regular church life. She shared that most of her community was online and filled with others doing the same things, so nothing felt off.

But everything changed in 2021. That was when Nina had just given birth to her first child. Her son ended up in the NICU, where she and her husband had to undergo the trauma of him flatlining three times.

"There was one point when he was flatlining, and they kicked us out of the room. Every nurse and doctor on the floor was in there trying to resuscitate him. You could hear the chest compressions through the door. In that moment, I was like,

What have I been doing? The only thing I had was the name of Jesus."

That moment was a spiritual turning point for Nina. She described it as a sudden clarity, a kind of awakening. From that day forward, she turned her back on everything: yoga, manifestation, crystals, and energy work. She began the process of repentance and healing. The road to freedom wasn't instant. It took about a year to find and remove objects from her home and walk through deliverance.

"There was a lot of demonic oppression I had to deal with. Spirits of confusion, anxiety, fear, depression, Kundalini, deception, witchcraft, all of it." Nina also reached out personally to her former clients and publicly repented. "The Lord had me call each of the clients I worked with, repent to them, and come out online and openly renounce everything. That's when people started telling me, 'I was praying for you. I was worried about you.'"

Today, Nina is certified in inner healing and deliverance ministry. She speaks from experience when she warns other Christian women about the dangers of yoga.

"I was that girl. I was doing yoga, calling myself a Christian, thinking it was harmless. But the more I did it, the more anxious and fearful I became. I kept thinking, 'I just need to do more yoga. I need a different crystal.' But there is only one true healer, and His name is Jesus Christ."

She explained that what yoga offers is a counterfeit to true healing. "You can drink from the toilet or from filtered water.

Yoga is the toilet—it looks like water, but it makes you sick. You may feel peace after a session, but you're being spiritually opened to more oppression."

When I asked Nina about yoga without the spiritual aspects, the kind without the chanting or spiritual elements, she did not hesitate. "Even the poses are ways of opening yourself up to different gods. You can stretch without practicing yoga. God created stretching. But yoga is not stretching."

Her advice for others is simple:

"Don't go around the Healer to get healing. That will only lead to more damage. Go straight to Jesus."

WHAT ARE THE ALTERNATIVES TO YOGA?

Stepping away from yoga doesn't mean you have to step away from movement, mobility, flexibility, strength, or cardio. There are life-giving alternatives that align with both your body's needs and your walk with Christ.

As a Christ-centered woman who desires to stretch, strengthen, and move your body, you can engage in various forms of exercise and stretching routines that do not incorporate yoga. I know it doesn't seem like it because it's so popular, but yoga has almost become synonymous with stretching in general. There is a certain vibe associated with those who practice it. A whole lifestyle has been built around yoga to draw in the health-conscious community. But think about this: everything associated with exercise is not yoga, but there seems to be only two camps for some reason – those who lift weights or those who practice yoga. When your doctor says you need to exercise, the following suggestion is usually yoga, or when your therapist suggests exercise as part of the treatment plan, the example that follows usually includes yoga.

Yoga is promoted everywhere: in stores, in the workplace, and even in schools as young as preschool. While yoga has roots in Hindu philosophy and spirituality, most Western yoga classes and programs emphasize only the physical and mental aspects of the practice rather than its religious or spiritual elements. This is a non-denominational approach to yoga to make it more palatable for secular settings such as schools and workplaces, where diversity of beliefs may exist. It sounds like proselytizing to me. So, how do you get away from it to just exercise?

When I realized what yoga actually was and decided to set it down, I felt a deep sense of loss. My first thought was, "What do I do now? How am I supposed to exercise, build strength, and have community?" I was sad. I didn't know what to do. I felt stuck. I have a strong feeling if I were to ask someone who has just gave up their yoga practice what other options are available to them, they might stare into the distance, unsure of how to respond. I can relate to that feeling.

But you know, one of the best things about being a Christian is that the Lord knows our hearts intimately. He is well-acquainted with our thoughts and reasonings. This isn't just a comforting notion; it's a reality. I will never forget sitting in the center of my couch, staring out into my little living room, and God spoke to me and said, "Yoga does not have the lock on exercise or movement." He met me right where I was, right in the middle of me trying to "figure this out." He gave me a plan moving forward.

I felt inspired to create a way of moving, stretching, and building strength that was free from an affiliation with yoga, which ultimately evolved into a brand. The brand became a way of being, and that is one of the motivating factors that inspired this book. I knew I wanted to honor God with my body, but as I contemplated what that would look like, I realized that ultimately I live to honor Him with my entire life. This realization led me to the name Flogos, which combines "flo" (meaning flowing) and "logos" (meaning the Word). It signifies flowing with the Word of God, and it's intended to encompass every area of your life, allowing God's Word to influence all aspects of life. It's a mindset, a reminder not just to read God's Word but apply it.

Looking back, the Lord took something I was doing that He was not pleased with and turned it into an opportunity for me to learn and share with others. This book is Him using my experience to help others. My experience also birthed a yoga alternative. He saw my heart and my desire to use yoga to help others; I loved my "exercise routine," and when God called me to lay yoga down, I didn't know where to turn to continue my health and wellness journey, but He knew all along. I look at this whole experience as a picture of Genesis 50:20 and Romans 8:28 in my life. God always has a bigger plan, and when we stay connected to His will we get to walk it out.

Where Can I Go?
Now what do I do? How will I exercise?

At the start of my journey, I felt restricted in choosing where to work out. I couldn't join any workout class because my eyes and ears were now open, and I was attuned to so much more than before, so group classes that merged any form of yoga into their sessions would just feel wrong. The poses weighed heavily on my mind, and I was afraid of putting my body into a position that dishonored God and went against everything He had just revealed to me. It makes sense that my newly opened eyes were cautious. While I didn't want to engage in anything related to yoga, I also understood that God wasn't asking me to live in fear of moving my body either.

So, how do you get away from yoga and still exercise?

If you're only stretching, you aren't doing yoga, right?

I want to make this clear because I don't want to cause fear with regard to bending your body. Yoga is only practiced within the broader context of its philosophy and principles. Therefore, stretch! Stretch, and stretch some more, and please breathe while doing so. Just don't practice yoga.

Remember, there are only so many ways to move the human body (seems obvious, right?). It's not something I'd ever thought about before this experience, but our bodies cannot move in an infinite number of ways. I share this because yoga and Hinduism do not own all the ways to move the body. If you want to stretch your hamstrings, increase flexibility, or deepen your splits, it is not yoga. Yoga is being led in a series of poses, breathing techniques, and/or meditations. That is intentionally practicing yoga.

Let me provide a real example: the most basic and common flow that anyone who has taken a yoga class has done is Sun Salutation A and B. The Sun Salutation sequences, both A and B, have roots in Hindu mythology and are dedicated to the Hindu sun god. Sun Salutation A is a simple flow of forward folds, plank, backbends, and Downward Dog. Sun Salutation B builds on Sun A by adding Chair Pose (like sitting in an invisible chair) and Warrior I. These two sequences are considered physical manifestations and are performed as a way to show honor.

What are some alternatives? There are alternatives to yoga, but you have to be careful because a lot of instructors just rename yoga poses and still teach full sequences straight out of a yoga class. Some will even place Christian or faith in the title, but it's still yoga. You can search for alternatives to yoga on YouTube, but I recommend doing some research before following any routine or taking a class. Here are some options to consider:

- Ballet, gymnastics, or mobility-inspired stretching routines
- Dance fitness classes, which provide a great cardio workout
- High-intensity interval training (HIIT)
- Outdoor or indoor activities such as hiking, biking, swimming, running, and rock climbing
- Strength training and weightlifting
- Simple stretching is always a good choice

Make sure to read the class description or inquire about the session to ensure it isn't blended with yoga. It can sometimes be challenging to differentiate between regular stretching and yoga since both involve some similar physical movements. However, there are several clear indicators that a stretching routine is influenced by yoga. One key sign is the strong emphasis on synchronizing breath with each movement, like a meditative flow, and sometimes there is the added prompt of everyone breathing together. Now, while most exercise programs will cue you to breathe, since we often hold our breath during strenuous activities, yoga places a greater emphasis on specific breathing patterns. Breathing is typically diaphragmatic, and usually includes techniques like Ujjayi breath. Other types of exercises focus on lateral breathing, where you expand the ribs outward, with the focus being on keeping the core engaged.

Another clue is the use of yoga-specific names, whether in English or Sanskrit, such as Downward Dog, Warrior I or II, and Tadasana. Additionally, yoga routines will usually follow a flow or sequence where poses transition smoothly from one to the next; while this isolated technique isn't an absolute sign of yoga, when combined with other indicators, it can help clarify the distinction. Furthermore, if the session incorporates elements of meditation, mindfulness, or a body scan, it is likely yoga-based. The presence of a spiritual or philosophical dimension, such as themes of gratitude, energy centers (chakras), or inner peace, also differentiates yoga from typical stretching. If some or all of these clues are present, it is a strong indication that you've been practicing yoga or a yoga-inspired routine. You don't need to know every yoga pose to recognize if a stretching routine incorporates yoga elements; you can just ask the instructor, and they will let you know if the class includes yoga practices. Lastly, if the instructor is a certified yoga instructor, their qualifications will be listed with how many hours of training they have completed, and that is a clear indication that it will be a yoga or yoga-inspired class.

OUTRO

My dear sisters in Christ, as you pursue health and wholeness, remember that your body is a temple of the Holy Spirit, and caring for it is both wise and Biblical, but so is guarding your heart and mind from deception. The New Age movement is prevalent in the health and wellness space and serves as a vehicle the enemy uses to disguise lies under the guise of peace, healing, and self-improvement. Not everything that appears good on the outside is from God. I learned this the hard way, but I am grateful to have the opportunity to share my journey with you.

Be discerning. Test every practice against the truth of Scripture, and seek the Lord in all things. Don't be afraid to move your body, but let His Word be your guide. You don't need to pursue Eastern philosophies or any spiritual practices outside of the Word of God to find peace or purpose. God's way is enough. Align your wellness journey with His truth, and you'll remain anchored in the only source that never changes. So be free to stretch and breathe, and move in ways that honor God without opening the door to spiritual compromise. Walk in truth, stand firm in His Word, and I pray that you let Him be the source of your peace and strength.

APPENDIX

Yoga Sutras

(The Yoga Sutras are divided into four chapters. Here is a brief breakdown of each)

Samadhi Pada (Chapter on Contemplation): This chapter introduces the concept of yoga and its ultimate goal of attaining a state of Samadhi. This is where a person feels completely one with the universe or the divine. It's a deep focus or meditation, where someone reaches a state beyond themselves and their thoughts. When you reach this point, you have "arrived." It's the point at which union with the divine is reached. Yoga means "to yoke" or "union." This is the union that the asanas (exercises) get you ready for.

Sadhana Pada (Chapter on Practice): This chapter outlines the practical side of yoga. It explains the eight limbs of yoga, called Ashtanga Yoga. This is the spiritual side of yoga. This is the path yogis take for spiritual growth and self-realization. These steps include things like being kind, the asanas (doing yoga exercises), controlling your breathing, focusing your mind, meditating, and finally, reaching Samadhi, the peaceful state where you feel one with the universe. Each limb represents a different aspect or stage of the yogic path.

Vibhuti Pada (Chapter on Accomplishments): This chapter explores the siddhis, attainments, or special powers one can reach through advanced yogic practices. These aren't about being really flexible or strong. The chapter says that if you practice yoga a lot, you might get powers like reading minds, seeing things that aren't there, or even floating! But it also reminds you to stay humble and pure, and not to focus too much on these powers. Instead, you should use them to help others, not for yourself.

Kaivalya Pada (Chapter on Liberation): This is the final chapter of the *Yoga Sutras*, and it's all about reaching the ultimate goal—freedom, or liberation. This means being completely free from the things that cause us to suffer. Patanjali explains that fluctuations of the mind can obscure one's true nature and perpetuate the cycle of suffering. According to Patanjali, learning to calm the mind by clearing the mind through meditation is how to break the cycle of suffering.

Types of Yoga

- **Karma Yoga** – The purpose is to develop a way of life that focuses on doing good deeds. Karma yoga is one way those who practice Hinduism grow spiritually.

- **Bhakti Yoga** – The purpose is devotion. This is one of the four main paths of yoga in Hindu philosophy that leads to the divine.

- **Jana Yoga** – The purpose is to unlock inner peace and clarity. The focus is the inner self, which is called the atman, becoming one with the ultimate truth and source of everything, called the Brahman in Hindu philosophy.

- **Kundalini Yoga** – The purpose is to release into the body the fire/serpent energy that is said to be coiled at the base of the spine. This is how you are supposed to develop psychic ability.

- **Mantra Yoga** – The purpose is audible & inaudible chanting or repetition of certain words and phrases that are used to steady the mind and create subtle transformation. The Sanskrit words are pronounced in very specific ways because they are said to have special power.

- **Hatha Yoga/Tantra Yoga** – The oldest form of yoga. The purpose is to join, yoke, or balance the sun and moon, the two opposing sides. This is a common yoga practiced in studios here in the States.

- **Ashtanga Yoga** – The sole purpose is to control and transcend the mind. This is one of the most common forms of yoga.

- **Power Yoga** – This is a westernized version of Ashtanga yoga.

- **Bikram Yoga** – This is hot yoga and is a style of hatha yoga.

What Yoga Poses Really Mean

If you're tracking with me, then you already know I "used to" look at the poses in yoga as merely exercises. However, I have shared that these poses are called "asanas," which are yoga postures intended to serve as a bridge to the other eight limbs of yoga. They are much more than just physical exercises. These postures go beyond physical alignment, flexibility, or exercise; they carry much deeper symbolic meanings tied to Hindu deities. When you attend a yoga class and position yourself in these poses, you are not only mimicking what Hindu gods are said to look like physically, but you are also using your body to convey a story that is being told.

Know that not all the postures done in a yoga class have a direct correlation to Hinduism. Here are three examples of poses that are used in the practice of yoga but have no origins in Hindu philosophy and tradition.

1. Mountain Pose

This is where you are standing still, facing forward with your feet together, arms at your sides, and your body is in alignment from head to toe. You raise your arms up in a mountain position, and you can even bend from side to side. This is a stretch. This is not practicing yoga.

2. Forward Bend

This is where you are standing still, facing forward with your feet hip-width apart, arms at your sides, and then you hinge at the hips, allowing your torso to move towards your legs. This stretch is not yoga.

3. Seated Forward Bend

This is where you sit on the floor with your legs stretched out in front of you and you hinge your hips, folding your upper body over your legs while reaching for your feet. This is stretching and is not considered yoga.

These poses are used both outside and inside of yoga practice. How many dancers, gymnasts, or athletes use these stretches with no ties to yoga? Lots! Although these and other stretches can easily be found in a yoga class, they are not, in and of themselves, considered actual yoga poses. These are actually just ways in which our body moves when being stretched. Many different professions utilize these exercises.

Then there are poses that are directly related to yoga, Hinduism, mythology, deities, and have a story behind them. These poses serve as physical expressions of devotion and reverence toward Hindu deities. Those who are really into their practice connect with the stories, qualities, and energies represented by these divine beings. Moving your body to stretch is not considered yoga. What turns it from stretching to yoga is the intention, the way the class is laid out, the poses, and the sequences in which the poses are done. I will only list a few examples, as there are many.

4. Virabhadrasana/the Warrior Poses (I, II, & III)

- **Warrior 1** – This is where you step into a lunge, your hips face forward as you lift your arms overhead, reaching up through your fingertips while grounding down through your feet.

- **Warrior 2** – This is the same stance as Warrior 1, but you open your hips and shoulders to the side and your arms extend out to the sides like a T (keeping them at shoulder height), reaching in both directions as you gaze over your front hand.

- **Warrior 3** – This is where you transition from Warrior 2 and balance on your front leg by leaning your torso forward and lifting your back leg behind you until your body forms a straight line from head to heel. Your arms can stretch forward, out to the sides, or reach back alongside your body as you stay strong through your standing leg.

In yoga, these three poses honor Virabhadra. This is one of those poses that isn't practiced outside of the context of yoga, and if it is, it's still called yoga, not stretching. In all my years of dance classes and sports, never have I encountered this stretch, so I would say this is one of those poses to steer clear of, as it is directly related to Hinduism. The warrior poses tell the story of a fierce warrior in Hindu mythology, Virabhadra, and depict a bloody murder; they are basically playing out a revenge execution between the gods.

The poses tell the story of the god Shiva and his wife, Sati. Sati's father, King Daksha, disapproved of their marriage, so he arranged a sacrificial ceremony and did not invite Shiva, his son-in-law. Sati pleaded with her father, but despite her pleas, she attended the ceremony alone, where her father insulted Shiva, her husband. Overcome with grief and rage at the disrespect shown to Shiva, Sati sacrificed herself in the fire. Then, in his sorrow and anger, Shiva tore a lock of hair from his head and threw it to the ground, where it transformed into Virabhadra, the warrior. Shiva then instructed the warrior to go and avenge Sati's death by disrupting her father's sacrificial ceremony and killing everyone present. Virabhadra went in wielding a sword and, accompanied by an army, stormed into the ceremony and confronted Sati's father, killing him and his guests and destroying the sacrificial site.

These postures and their sequences have a direct correlation to the practice of yoga, but if you step into a lunge on its own, you stretch your arms wide out to the sides, or stand on one leg to test your balance, you are not doing yoga, nor are you playing out the scene described above. Yoga isn't just creating shapes with your body; it's how you move, the sequences you use, in some cases how you breathe, and why you're there. Practicing yoga takes intention.

5. Ardha Chandrasana or the Half Moon Pose:

This is where you balance on one leg while reaching the same-side hand down toward the floor, stacking your hips as you lift your other leg out to the side. Your top arm stretches up toward the sky, and your chest opens as you gaze up.

The pose is named after Chandra, the Hindu god of the moon. The pose is believed to evoke qualities of balance, serenity, and lunar energy. This pose can be either bound or unbound.

6. Natarajasana or the Lord of the Dance Pose:

This is where you stand tall on one leg while bending your leg behind you to reach back with one hand and grab the inside of your other foot to lift it behind you. You lean forward and you stretch your free arm forward. Your body forms a curve, like a bow that's being drawn.

The pose is named after Nataraja, another form of the Hindu god Shiva. It represents the continuous cycle of creation, preservation, and destruction in the universe.

7. Matsyasana or the Fish Pose:

This is where you start by lying on your back with your legs extended out in front of you and your arms resting (touching the sides of your body). You then press your forearms into the floor and lift your chest to arch your upper back as you let the crown of your head rest on the ground.

This pose is named after Matsya, who is the fish incarnation of the Hindu god Vishnu. This pose is believed to symbolize salvation and rebirth, reflecting the mythological story of Vishnu's manifestation as a fish to save the world from a great flood.

8. Hanumanasana or the Monkey Pose:

This is where you lower down into a full split. One leg is reaching forward, and the other is stretching back behind you.

This pose is named after the Hindu deity Hanuman. Practicing this pose is a way of honoring Hanuman's qualities and seeking inspiration from his mythological feats. It may seem like just doing the splits, but in yoga, it is not. If you look it up, you'll see it's "similar" to the splits. The shape may be the same, but in yoga, it's not looked at as just the splits; it is a part of a story.

REFERENCES

Bible Versions Used:

1. AMP (Amplified Bible): The Holy Bible: Amplified Bible. 2015. Grand Rapids: Zondervan.

2. AMPC (Amplified Bible, Classical Edition): The Holy Bible: Amplified Bible, Classical Edition, 1965/2015. La Habra, CA: The Lockman Foundation.

3. ESV (English Standard Version): The Holy Bible: English Standard Edition, 2001/2016. Wheaton, IL: Crossway/Good News Publishers.

4. NIV (New International Version): The Holy Bible: New International Version. 1984. Grand Rapids: Zondervan.

5. NKJV (New King James Version): The Holy Bible: New King James Version. 1982. Nashville: Thomas Nelson.

6. NLT (New Living Translation): Holy Bible: New Living Translation. Tyndale House Publishers, 2015.

7. TPT (The Passion Translation): The Holy Bible: The Passion Translation. 2017. Lake Mary, FL: BroadStreet Publishing Group.

Yoga Teacher Training Through A Biblical World View

1. Yoga St. Louis. "Patanjali Invocation – Yoga St. Louis." Yoga St. Louis, 1 Sept. 2016, yogastlouis.us/resources/patanjali-invocation.

2. Satchidananda, Sri Swami. The *Yoga Sutras* of Patanjali: Translation and Commentary. Integral Yoga Publications, 1978.

3. Merriam-Webster. (n.d.). Namaste. In Merriam-Webster. com dictionary. Retrieved September 25, 2024 from https:// www.merriam-webster.com/dictionary/namaste

So What Is Yoga Then

1. Iyengar, B.K.S. Light on Yoga. Schocken Books, 1966.

2. Ugly Delicious. Directed by, Eddie Schmidt, Jason Zeldes, Laura Gabbert, & Morgan Neville, 2020. Netflix app.

3. Sri Swami Satchidananda, The *Yoga Sutras* of Patanjali: Translation and Commentary, Incantation (Buckingham, VA: Integral Yoga Publications, 1978)

4. Kempton, Sally. "Seeds of Change: Yogic Understanding of Karma." Yoga Journal, updated 16 Jan. 2025, www.yogajournal.com/lifestyle/seeds-change/.

Is There Such A Thing As Christian Yoga

1. Satchidananda, Sri Swami. The *Yoga Sutras* of Patanjali: Translation and Commentary. Integral Yoga Publications, 1978.

2. Christian Yoga Association. "Christian Yoga Association." Christian Yoga Association, https://christianyogaassociation.org/. Accessed 2 Jan. 2025.

3. The School of the Natural Order. School of the Natural Order, www.sno.org/. Accessed 25 Sept. 2024.

4. "Yoga fun facts." Yogi Times, February 2025, www.yogitimes.com/article/unstoppable-trend-yoga-infographic-business. Accessed 01 March. 2025.

5. Deborah Adele, The Yamas and Niyamas: Exploring Yoga's Ethical Practice (Duluth, MN: On-Word Bound Books, 2009)

6. "Namaste." Merriam-Webster.com Dictionary, Merriam-Webster, www.merriam-webster.com/dictionary/namaste. Accessed 25 Sept. 2024.

Close Open Doors

1. Virtue, Doreen. "An A-Z List of New Age Practices to Avoid, and Why." Doreen Virtue, 21 July 2019, doreenvirtue.com/2019/07/21/an-a-z-list-of-new-age-practices-to-avoid-and-why/.

2. Sobel, Rabbi Jason. "Hebrew Letters and Numbers." Fusion with Rabbi Jason, Fusion Global, course, Thinkific, accessed 29 May 2025, fusionglobal.thinkific.com/courses/letters-and-numbers-v1.

3. Montenegro, Marcia. "Astral Travel and The Bible." Christian Answers for the New Age. https://www.christiananswersnewage.com/article/astral-travel-and-the-bible

4. "Astrology." Merriam-Webster.com Dictionary, Merriam-Webster, https://www.merriam-webster.com/dictionary/astrology. Accessed 29 May 2025.

5. Fauvre, Katherine. Disseminations of the Enneagram of Personality – Overview. Katherine Fauvre Consulting, www.katherinefauvre.com/dissemination-of-enneagram. Accessed 29 May. 2025.

6. Claudio Naranjo – 'Healing Civilization' – Interview by Eleonora Gilbert. YouTube, uploaded by conscioustv, Dec 21, 2010, https://www.youtube.com/watch?v=WynV-C9iPgM.

7. "Automatic Writing." Enneagram Interview, uploaded by YouTube, accessed 29 May. 2025, www.youtube.com/watch?v=wlO3KJWnNd8.

8. The Editors of Encyclopaedia Britannica. "Automatic Writing." Encyclopaedia Britannica, Encyclopaedia Britannica, Inc., accessed 29 May 2025, https://www.britannica.com/topic/automatic-writing.

9. Hogue, Elizabeth Rowley. "A Grand Rising." Awakening Ways, 1 Feb. 2024. Awakening Ways, https://awakeningways.org/a-grand-rising/. Accessed 29 May. 2025.

10. Got Questions Ministries. (n.d.). What does the Bible say about smudging? GodQuestions.org. https://www.gotquestions.org/Bible-smudging.html

11. "Superstition." Merriam-Webster.com Dictionary, Merriam-Webster, https://www.merriam-webster.com/dictionary/superstition. Accessed 24 Aug. 2025.

Pruning Self-Reliance

1. "Self-reliance." The Free Dictionary, American Heritage® Roget's Thesaurus, Houghton Mifflin Harcourt Publishing Company, 2013–14, www.thefreedictionary.com/self-reliance. Accessed 31 July. 2025.

Breathwork Vs Deep Breathing Exercises

1. B.K.S. Iyengar, Light on Yoga (New York: Schocken Books, 1966)

2. "Madonna Gives Up Exercise for Yoga." YouTube, uploaded by AP Archive, 1998, www.youtube.com/watch?v=dg41qSGa5vI. Accessed 16 Sept. 2023.

Yoga Sutras

1. Satchidananda, Sri Swami. The *Yoga Sutras* of Patanjali: Translation and Commentary. Integral Yoga Publications, 1978.

What Yoga Poses Really Mean

1. Lall, Ashley. "Spiritual Meanings of Yoga Postures." Livestrong, 1 Dec. 2022, www.livestrong.com/article/395082-spiritual-meanings-of-yoga-postures/. Accessed 2 Jan. 2025.

ABOUT THE AUTHOR

 Ebony Clayton is a Licensed Clinical Social Worker, Coach, and Certified Group Fitness Instructor. She is a passionate truth seeker with a heart for helping women align their lives wholly with God's Word.

In "Mind Body Spirit - God's Way" Ebony invites readers into her personal testimony of awakening, discernment, and freedom, while shedding light on subtle deceptions in the culture, using her exposure to yoga as a prime example.

Ebony is working to create a space where women can embrace healthy living (physically, mentally, and emotionally) while staying grounded in their Christian faith. This vision is to provide a refuge from the New Age influences that have inundated our culture inspired FLogos, a wellness concept that blends "Flo" with "Logos".

Ebony lives in sunny Florida with her husband and daughter, where she homeschools, runs her Christian counseling practice, and continues to share her story to encourage those seeking the truth in a world filled with spiritual noise.